Deadheads and Christians

Deadheads and Christians

You Will Know Them By Their Love

Thomas A. Coogan

RESOURCE *Publications* · Eugene, Oregon

DEADHEADS AND CHRISTIANS
You Will Know Them By Their Love

Resource Publications
An Imprint of Wipf and Stock Publishers
199 W. 8th Ave., Suite 3
Eugene, OR 97401

www.wipfandstock.com

PAPERBACK ISBN: 979-8-3852-4059-3
HARDCOVER ISBN: 979-8-3852-4060-9
EBOOK ISBN: 979-8-3852-4061-6

VERSION NUMBER 04/04/25

Contents

List of Tables

Acknowledgments

I am grateful to the entire community of Nassau Presbyterian Church for guiding me to a modern, mature faith. In particular I am indebted to Rev. Joyce MacKichan Walker for setting me on a course of a serious approach to Scripture and for providing a forum where I could develop the ideas collected in this work. Dr. Mark Edwards, while on the Nassau Church staff, gave me sufficient prodding and encouragement to undertake the project it has now become. The Bible study group led by Rev. Dr. George Hunsinger has been invaluable to me, especially the three years spent poring over every detail of the book of the Acts of the Apostles. More recently, my efforts have greatly benefited from the input and feedback of numerous church members who were the first to affirm that there were valuable ideas to be explored here. Debbie Tegarden has provided unflagging enthusiasm, and Tom Charles made certain that every comma, was in its proper place.

On the Grateful Dead side, I am forever in debt to my older siblings who first exposed me to the band and who, along with younger family members, have been constant conversation partners on the topic. For showing me what "mature" Deadheads look and act like, I very much appreciate the online community at Dead.net, especially that group that came together in Chicago in 2015. Now officially known as the Sunshine Daydreamers, they will always be affectionately known in our family as the Watermelon Gang.

Acknowledgments

Finally in relation to this project, and for everything in my life, I owe more than I can say to my dear wife, Beth, whose mid-life adoption of the Dead lifestyle is the inspiration for this book.

Introduction

On June 21, 2023, Federal Reserve Chairman Jerome Powell, while testifying at a hearing of the Financial Services Committee of the United States House of Representatives, was asked by Rep. Wiley Nickel (D-NC) about reports that he had been seen at a recent Dead and Company concert. Chairman Powell happily confirmed that he had been at the event, added that he had thoroughly enjoyed it, and went on to say that he had been a fan of Grateful Dead music for fifty years. Rep. Nickel's reaction to the news was this blanket statement: "I like people who like the Grateful Dead."[1]

This exchange illustrates two salient points about a remarkable cultural phenomenon. The first is that the rock band that was synonymous with the counterculture of the 1960s is today embraced by individuals at the center of the US power structure, even unto the pinnacle of the capitalist economy. This is not because the entire audience at Dead shows has become, like Chairman Powell, the picture of conformity to cultural standards. On the contrary, a first-time visitor to a Dead and Company event will likely be impressed by the robustness of the subculture that continues to subsist in the manner of the original itinerant Deadheads. In fact, one of the most fascinating elements of the phenomenon is the clear evidence that these disparate groups, the upper echelon of society and those that sleep on the ground, are only too happy to mingle with one another at their tribal gatherings.

1. Roeloffs, "Deadhead at Heart," para. 4.

Introduction

The second striking takeaway from the Powell exchange is Congressman Nickel's sweeping declaration of being favorably disposed toward Deadheads. That statement itself had two components: first, it is possible to generalize about characteristics shared by Deadheads, beyond their taste in music; and second, these characteristics are positive ones. It is assumed that the concept of the Deadhead has become so familiar it does not need to be defined here. They have been discussed on and off in the popular press over several decades. The caravan of traveling fans has reliably provided material for colorful copy and intriguing images in countless news reports. This was again the case when the popular summer tours of Dead and Company made them a topic of discussion, even in congressional committee hearings.

This book is about Deadheads and their shared characteristics. Its purpose is to persuade those who profess the Christian faith to get to know some in the other group and, in the course of doing so, to test whether or not what is claimed in this book is true: that, in their fundamental attitudes about life, Christians and Deadheads have a great deal in common. Given the availability of Deadheads throughout the land, this work will draw on their generally friendly nature as a resource to prove its claims. Each chapter of this work includes a claim about a characteristic shared by Deadheads; the reader is encouraged to test the universal nature of these attributes by engaging Deadheads in dialogue.

In addition to assuming that readers are familiar with the term Deadhead, it is also assumed that the reader will have no difficulty in making the acquaintance of at least one. Suggesting that readers will not face a challenge in asking Deadheads about their common characteristics makes two initial generalizations about them. The first is that Deadheads do not hesitate to let others know this aspect of their identity. If the reader is already friendly with someone with that affiliation, it's a good bet that this topic has already come up. The second generalization about Deadheads is that they will be open and generous in discussing the nature of Deadheads with someone who approaches them in a kind spirit. This is in fact the first characteristic, attached to this section of the book, which readers can test: Deadheads are open and engaging toward new acquaintances. Should anyone encounter any difficulty in approaching a Deadhead, they should be able to break the ice with a reminder of the song lyric from "Scarlet Begonias" about stopping a stranger just to exchange a greeting.

The premise of this work is that, as Christians engage with Deadheads, they will discover an expanding common ground as each generalization proves true. Christians (and other nonaffiliated readers of this work) might find that Deadheads are a population of unexpected allies in our society. People of faith might come to regard Deadheads as a group that must be *for us*, since they are not against us, as is described in the Gospels (Mark 9:40). This can be the case even if the Deadheads state that they do not hold a favorable opinion of organized religion, as some no doubt will, and can never be expected to darken the door of a church. It can still be the case that the Deadheads' style of living is consonant with that recommended in the Gospels.

Though this work is by a Christian and written for a Christian target audience, it is in no way meant to imply that there is any exclusiveness in the allied attitudes between Christian believers and Deadheads. As much as the Golden Rule has parallels in other faith traditions, so do all people of good will have commonalities with the open, trusting, and generous spirit that is characteristic of Deadheads.

Each of the attributes being attributed to Deadheads in this work could be viewed as one node in a twelve-point Venn diagram—none of these are in any way exclusive to Deadheads. It would make no more sense to say that "all Deadheads are baseball fans" than to say, "all baseball fans are Deadheads." That caveat is easily accepted, and yet it still remains true that it can be instructive to consider the degree of overlap between the groups.

The point must be emphasized, and will be repeatedly, that this work is not intending to posit a one-to-one relationship between the attitudes of Christians and Deadheads. The intent is strictly to comment on common, positive characteristics. No slight is meant to the faith tradition, or lack thereof, of any Deadhead.

Particularly it should be noted that the ranks of Deadheads have included significant numbers of Jews since the earliest days. By no means is any offense, or exclusivity, intended by suggesting that Deadheads, as a group, share common traits with Christians. In these days when the connotations of the term "Christian" have been changing in the US, that terminology might especially chafe. When drawing comparisons to Deadheads, the term Christian is used here in the traditional, peace-and-love sense, not the guns-and-bigotry politicization that has recently surrounded it.

If there is any instruction to be drawn from making these comparisons, it is not that Deadheads should, or inevitably will, become more Christian. On the contrary, if there are lessons to be learned, it is hoped that church-going people will be reminded of the Jewish origins of their Scripture and earliest practices. A Christianity that is allied with the most powerful in society seems adrift from the ways of the preacher from Nazareth who had no end of conflict with the religious hierarchy of his day. Or, to put it more directly, the suggestion is not that Deadheads become more like Christians, rather, it is that Christians, as a group, become more like Deadheads.

There are many published works on the history of the Grateful Dead as a band, on the individual band members, and their body of musical output. This work does not add to that collection. This work is about the fans of the band, their characteristics and their evolution. Just as the apostle Luke began his two-part work on the Jesus movement with an acknowledgment that many others had already written about the primary events (Luke 1:1), so in the present circumstance, we find that there is yet more to explore as the Deadhead movement continues to flourish. What is said here about the movement can be understood without ever listening to any of the music (though it would help). The focus here is on the observable features of the Deadhead movement without reference to the content that binds them to one another. Imagine a circumstance in which you might observe the behavior of everyone in attendance at a Dead event without hearing any of the music.

Introduction

The idea that there are elements of religion in the Grateful Dead phenomenon is one that has been explored from many perspectives. This work has a narrow focus: just as this book does not deal at all with the music itself neither does it examine in detail the song lyrics at the core of the movement. There are clear parallels between those lyrics and various sacred writings, but no further commentary on that topic will be offered. The approach taken here is akin to asking: What would contemporary observers, with no exposure to the Gospel writings, have said about the early Christians?

To facilitate the goal of fostering dialogue between Christians and Deadheads, two common elements are included in each chapter. In addition to the generalizations about Deadheads that can be tested in dialogue, each chapter includes quotes from Scripture. The Scripture passages are principally from the writings about the early Christian community, after the time of the gospel stories. One source is the Acts of the Apostles, the historical record of the early movement. These are used to provide some comparison to the Deadhead movement in terms of the facts and figures of what took place. Besides the historical record, which has its limitations, there are other writings to and about the early Christians (the Epistles). These provide a fuller picture of common attitudes of people in the community, commenting on what the attributes of believers are, and/or what they should be. In these passages a more direct comparison can be made between the ways of Christians and the ways of Deadheads, separate from the historical parallel of the growth and evolution of movements.

By highlighting the early Scripture, the intent is to refocus the notion of what a Christian is back on their common behaviors and attitudes. These were the defining elements of the faith long before there were debates on practices (for instance, the how, when, and where of partaking of the sacraments). As a first example, consider this simple statement of what it means to adopt a Christian attitude, one that could be embraced by any Deadhead: "Don't act from selfishness or pride, but in humility count others as superior to yourself; look not to your own interest but those of others" (Phil 2:3–4).

I

Parallels Between the Dead and Company Era and Events in Acts of the Apostles

The passage: "If it be of man it will fail, but if it be of God . . ." (Acts 5:38–39).[1]

The context: The religious authorities of Jesus' time were presented with a conundrum: despite their best efforts to shut it down, Jesus' movement continued to flourish in his absence. At a council meeting, as recorded in Acts, one leader, named Gamaliel, advised the authorities to exercise a little humility and recall that divine action may not always be easy to recognize, though it be right before their eyes.

✝

---

1. All Scripture translations are by the author. Readers with concerns about their accuracy are encouraged to compare to their preferred version. Better yet, compare to two or three versions. Even better still, check the Greek.

A movement that began as itinerants, living hand to mouth at the fringes of society and referring to one another as brother and sister, continues to grow nearly thirty years after the death of its leader. A new generation, born after the death of the leader, has begun to replenish the ranks of the itinerant true believers, even as broader segments of society participate in the community's gatherings.

That description is meant to apply equally well to the early days of the Jesus movement as to the current stage of the Deadhead movement. By pointing out their parallel developments, the intent here is to open the eyes of current Jesus followers to a growing movement that deserves to be taken seriously. It does not, however, in any way, intend to draw comparisons between the founders of the two movements; this topic will be addressed more fully in chapter 6.

THE CENTRAL ANALOGY

The idea that the Deadhead movement resembles a religious movement is not a new one. Comments to that effect, from those inside and by outside observers, have been made from its earliest days. The goal of this work is to be explicit in examining the attributes of this movement and draw comparisons to the attributes reported about the Jesus movement in its earliest days, long before its beliefs and practices were codified into the church of later centuries.

An analogy in the style of old SAT questions will provide a meaningful perspective on how the current Deadhead phenomenon relates to the original Grateful Dead fan base: Dead and Company is to the Grateful Dead what the Acts of the Apostles are to the Gospels. More accurately, it should be stated that the time period in which Dead and Company has been active is parallel to the time period covered in the Acts of the Apostles.

The writer who produced both the book of the Acts of the Apostles and the Gospel of Luke (whose name is unknown)[2] linked those two works by beginning each with a comment

---

2. See Gaventa, introduction to *Acts of the Apostles*, 2056–58.

addressed to a "Theophilus." These two works are presented as part 1 and part 2 of an unfolding story (see Acts 1:1). Part 1 ends with instructions that the message be spread to all peoples of the Earth (Luke 24:47); part 2 picks up just after Jesus had left the earth and covers the time period up to and including when the apostle Paul was established in the city of Rome.

TIME FOR A NEW ASSESSMENT

The inspiration for this book is the recognition that a critical stage has been passed by the Deadhead phenomenon, and so this is an appropriate time to reevaluate the idea that it resembles a religious movement. The writer of Acts ended that work with Paul spreading his message in Rome, and the underlying theme of that entire work was to show how they arrived at that point. The writer, of course, knew that was the outcome, and the past events, which led up to that point, were evaluated and presented with that understanding. This work takes as its endpoint the occasion of the Fed Chair discussing Dead and Company in congressional testimony, inviting comparison to Paul's arrival in Rome as an historical corollary.

The work of the writer of Acts (as well as writers of other later Gospels) reflects the fact that they had seen their movement pass major milestones. In that knowledge, they felt confident that the movement would continue to flourish. Likewise, our current perspective is one of a new period in which the longevity of the Deadhead movement is assured. With Dead and Company now having completed their tenth year of very successful concerts, the time is ripe for a new assessment of the state of the movement and its significance. That there remains such palpable vitality nearly thirty years after the death of Jerry Garcia has to prompt a serious reevaluation of how this has happened.

SPREAD IN THE ABSENCE OF CENTRAL CONTROL

The references at the end of the book of Acts to Paul being established in Rome should not be confused with the later role that Rome, in the form of the church hierarchy, played in shaping and controlling the Jesus movement. In fact, one of the salient features of the early phases of the Jesus movement is that it occurred without coordinated (human) direction. The history as it is recounted in Acts (which does not match other records in every particular), is of growth in diverse forms and directions. Disagreements about the nature of the movement were rife and were reported in Acts and battled out in the Epistles. The debates about the nature of the founder of the movement went on for hundreds of years.

The evangelists' stories consistently report that they encountered believers over widespread areas. It is clear that the Jesus message was being propagated from sources other than from the core faithful based in Jerusalem. On his missionary road trips, for example, Paul found communities of Jesus followers who had heard a gospel that did not match the one that he had learned. His missionary partners, Aquila and Priscilla, encountered another preacher who was "mighty in Scripture" but knew only the baptism of John. This fellow, Apollos of Alexandria, needed further instruction in the way of Jesus to support his preaching (Acts 18:24–26). These were not isolated occurrences: in the very next episode in Acts, Paul encounters believers in Ephesus who knew of John's baptism but were entirely unfamiliar with the notion of a Holy Spirit. Paul corrects this with a quick laying on of hands, which promptly results in prophesying and speaking in tongues. The writer of Acts adds the detail that there were "about twelve" in this group at Ephesus (Acts 19:1–7).

A wide variety of written witnesses were produced in the early days of the Jesus movement, as referenced in Luke 1:1. It was only over many decades that this collection was culled down to a small canon of authorized writings. It took even longer, hundreds of years, for agreement to be reached on a comprehensive understanding of the movement, and even now this is not unanimous.

The varieties of surviving Christian churches (Syriac, Coptic, Orthodox) belie the idea that there ever was anything monolithic in the Jesus movement, and this was all long before the flourishing of church types that was set off by the Reformation. As much as it is true today, so it was then: the earliest days of the Jesus movement were anything but homogeneous.

UNCOORDINATED PROLIFERATION OF THE DEAD PHENOMENON

In the world of Deadheads, the success of Dead and Company concert tours marked an important milestone and touchstone but is only the most prominent element in a broad universe of Dead-related activity. A key observation about the wide variety of expression in the Deadhead movement is its organic, home-grown nature as opposed to something that is the product of a record company promotional effort. Its dimensions and manifestations are more fully detailed in chapter 2; the present point is its parallel to the undirected growth of the Jesus movement.

Before Dead and Company came along there were the many permutations in combinations of original band members playing together (Furthur, The Dead, The Other Ones). Original band member Phil Lesh has continued to chart his own course independent of the others, touring on a smaller scale with Phil and Friends, even as Dead and Company filled stadiums and drew headlines. In due time, of course, there will not be any surviving members left around to perform at rock concerts. All of the evidence shows, however, that those original band members can have absolute assurance that there will continue to be fans in those future days who will go to performances of their music after they are gone. That is where the cover bands come in.

Outside of the realm of the surviving band member are the uncounted varieties of cover bands dedicated to live performances of Grateful Dead music. They perform shows that, according to published setlists, are not distinguishable from the "authorized" versions at shows put on by surviving band members. The point is not that there is a standard by which to make a distinction between orthodox and unapproved versions of performance. The significance of the proliferation of bands playing Grateful Dead music is that the movement has its own momentum.

An analogy from the world of cosmology may be helpful (real science cosmology, not the kind practiced at Dead shows). Most modern people will be familiar with the notion that the universe is expanding; fewer may be aware of the more recent idea that the rate of expansion is accelerating. Common notions of the Big Bang as the source of the expanding universe give the impression that the expansion would in time decelerate, something like the remnants of a fireworks explosion slowly drifting after the initial burst. The latest interpretation of data on the behavior of galaxies is that the expansion of the universe is occurring at an accelerating rate, not slowing.[3] Evidence of accelerating expansion has required new hypotheses to be developed, which suggest the existence of a (still poorly understood) dark energy of some sort that is driving the continued expansion. Likewise, there seems to be something driving further expansion in the numbers and enthusiasm of those who attend jam-band festivals to hear Grateful Dead and Dead-style music.

RAPID SPREAD BY NEW MEANS

The twin stars of the book of Acts, the apostles Peter and Paul (sorry, no Mary after the first chapter), were both reported to marvel at how believers were being made among people and in places that they would not have expected. All of their accounts of new conversions report that they take place through direct personal interactions. But that would change.

As already mentioned, in the opening to Luke's Gospel he comments on the proliferation of other writings on the same topic that he was taking up. Despite that statement used for setting a context, nowhere in Acts is there any further mention of any other

---

3. Bassi, "Universe Is Expanding."

writings. For all of the action in Acts that revolves around Paul, his letters, which did so much to spread the faith, are never described there, neither the writing of them nor any mention of anyone receiving them. In Acts, everyone who hears the good news that was coming out of Galilee got it by direct personal contact with someone else who had heard it. Though not mentioned in Acts, the written word would of course become the principal means by which the message was spread to peoples far removed in distance and time from the original events (though it is likely still true today that people do not become Christian simply through reading the texts without also having close contact with another believer).

The Deadhead movement, just as surely as the Jesus movement, is now gaining new adherents by means that are quite different from how it was in the early days. Originally, of course, there were just the live concerts and albums released by the band. As there was very little radio airplay of the Grateful Dead, almost all exposure to them happened through a direct personal connection to someone who was already a fan. That propagation through personal contact was greatly amplified by the introduction of new technology in the form of cassette tapes. Suddenly, recordings of concerts could be used to reproduce and spread the music (again, an organic activity not controlled or directed by the band or music industry).

Any analogy can be pushed too far, so here goes: early Christian writings on scrolls gave way to the codex (book) form, and music cassettes have in due course given way to the technology that has touched virtually every aspect of modern life. The internet has served as a powerful, prolific means of distributing Dead music and reaching new potential converts. The ranks of Deadheads are being replenished by enthusiasts who have come to the movement long after Jerry, and yet are as committed as any Deadhead has ever been (detailed in chapters 5 and 6).

A MOVEMENT WITH SELF-AWARENESS

The comparability of the Dead and Company time period to that of the later Scripture writings is much more than just the number of decades that have passed since the movement began. The writers of Acts and John's Gospel wrote in the assured knowledge that the movement they were part of had both a secure foundation and a path to growth that would continue to play out long after the writers' own life. The way the writers presented the founding events of the movement are colored by their understanding of how it would all turn out (or at least as far into the future as they would be able to see).

New converts are essential to any movement if it is to persist and not simply wither away. As the Jesus movement changed and grew, the participation of new members, who had no experience with the original events, were noticed by the later evangelists and became an important topic in their writing. John's Gospel, the last to be written, puts particular emphasis on the later joiners as the vital source of longevity.

Two examples from John's Gospel are used to highlight the ways in which knowledge of the success of the movement influenced how the past was presented to the readers. Chapter 5 of this work includes a discussion of a story familiar to nearly everyone: the risen Jesus tells doubting Thomas that in the coming days there will be those who do believe even though they were not there to see what Thomas had seen. At the time this was written, nearly all the believers would have been those who did not experience for themselves what had taken place in Galilee.

Another example is explored more fully here and relates directly to one of Jesus' simplest but most significant teachings: that his followers should love another (how that specific use of the word "love" relates to the Deadhead movement is explored in chapter 7). Jesus told his followers that others, the nonbelievers, would recognize them as part of his movement based on the love that they showed for one another; he said it would define them (John 13:35). When this was committed to writing, it was not a prediction but was written in light of what was already known to be true about the flourishing movement.

These two examples show the transition that was taking place toward writing specifically about the Jesus movement itself, not just the events and teachings that began it. The book of Acts had already begun a process that would then continue through the decades and centuries, and by which the study of Christianity itself became an important topic.

SELF-AWARENESS IN THE DEADHEAD MOVEMENT

As much as it was true that the later writers of the Jesus movement were influenced by the knowledge of its success, so it is with the state of the Deadhead movement as it comes to the end of the Dead and Company era (if reports are to be believed that it is ending). The performers and the crowd are in a position of knowing with absolute confidence that this movement, far from approaching its demise, is ascendant. Whether there is actual continued growth taking place, as opposed to very slow decline, is a question investigated in chapter 4. But at minimum every Deadhead is heartened by the knowledge that there will continue to be new Dead music, whether live or released from the recording vaults, for them to appreciate for as long as they live.

As each year passes, the role of the self-awareness of the movement is enhanced, but it was also evident from very early on. Chapter 11 highlights how much the lyrics of Robert Hunter were deeply influenced by the movement that he was part of. For the performers today, and over the more recent decades, the flourishing of the movement imbues all their performances with a different kind of relevance.

"THEY LOVE EACH OTHER"

The book of Acts ends in Rome, where converts are beginning to appear, and John's Gospel says that the believers will be recognized by their mutual love. These threads were combined in the next milestone of longevity when, instead of writing in Greek, the *lingua franca* of the ancient Mediterranean world, commentators began to write about the Christian movement in Latin, the official language of the empire. One of the first to do so was Tertullian (160–225) and one of his most quotable phrases echoes John's message. Tertullian wrote that the non-Christians around them, those in the majority, would be moved to comment about those in the faith: "Look . . . how they love one another."[4]

Tertullian was not an unbiased observer. He was a believer and was industrious in perpetuating the new sect. The great tracts that he produced were intended to reconcile the good and great of Roman society to the strange, upstart group that was making itself known.

A comparable mixture of commentary and advocacy can be seen in the Deadhead community today. From the beginning, the songwriters and performers were conscious of and commented on the Deadhead phenomenon as it took shape. They had a sense of something built to last, something which would not fade away. Now, in turn, the Deadheads are exerting their influence over the band. The very longevity of the movement, and the crowd's awareness of what they are part of, leads to certain songs being reinterpreted as making reference to the movement and its future.

Several examples are presented in chapter 12 of a crowd's reaction to songs having a meaning specific to the context of the movement. One prominent example is the popular song "Touch of Grey" with its rousing refrain about the persistence to overcome any obstacle. The connotations of that have changed over the decades, as will be discussed. More relevant to the early Christian writings is the song "They Love Each Other." On a surface level the topic might be seen as referring to a couple's romantic love. Today it is embraced in concert venues as the anthem of all the Deadheads, who, just as was said of Jesus followers, are known for their mutual affection. It is that all-important shared trait of the two communities that gives this work its title.

---

4. Tertullianus, *Apologeticus* 39.7, quoted in *Oxford Essential Quotations*, 4th ed. (2017), s.v. "Tertullian," 179.

The Deadhead trait: Deadheads have themselves said, or heard another say, that the Grateful Dead is like "my religion."

The comment: Though this trait is presented at the beginning of this book, it is not likely to be a good topic on which to start a conversation with a Deadhead. The traits attached to later chapters are more suitable for getting acquainted. For this one to be a fruitful topic, you should have a firm idea, before asking, of what you would consider to be the elements, in attitude and practices, of a legitimate religion. And bear in mind these words of Scripture: "Don't snuff out the Spirit. Do not disregard prophetic messages" (1 Thess 5:19–20).

2

The Deadhead Phenomenon

The passage: "About three thousand were added on that day . . ."
(Acts: 2:41).

The context: The book of Acts includes more presentation of facts
and figures than do the Gospels, which focus on the story, or the
Epistles, which are principally concerned with theology. A case in
point is this reference to the number of individuals converted on a
particular occasion of Peter's preaching. The Gospel writers would
normally refer only to a "crowd" of followers without providing
further detail (the loaves and fishes events being the notable excep-
tions). Following the example of Acts, this current chapter will try
to present "just the facts" about the scope of the Deadhead movement without touching much on its ethos. There is something to
be gained, though, by considering the exact language of the Scripture passage above. In light of the discussion (in later chapters) of
what constitutes a Deadhead, it is interesting to think a minute on
what it meant, in the days of the first apostles, to be "added" to the
movement on a particular occasion. Surely it did not mean signing
up for adherence to a complex system of practices, beliefs, creeds,
or catechism. In this passage, "being added" sounds like just about

the same level of commitment of those fans who report that they suddenly "get it" at a particular Dead show.

✝

The premise of this work is that any Christians who engage Deadheads in conversation will discover some meaningful common ground and that they will be enriched by the experience. For that proposition to be practical and worth pursuing depends on there being a sufficient number of Deadheads around—enough to be easily found, and enough that they constitute a significant sub-population of society that merits recognition. This chapter is the least theologically grounded in the book as it sets out to address those necessary conditions of there being a not-insignificant number of Deadheads about. What follows are data which indicate the numbers of Deadheads there are out there, as well as evidence that they are not fading away. This is worth noting, not only for the practical reality of their being easy to find, but also because it makes the point that there is something at work here which is unlike other run-of-the-mill fan groups. That idea will be more fully explored in chapter 4.

Readers who would like to learn about Deadheads firsthand will not have any difficulty finding them or engaging them in conversation. The idea that Deadheads are not difficult to find is based on the evidence that

a. there are plenty of them around;

b. they make themselves known;

c. and they congregate in places where it is easy to find them.

Later chapters will cover the topics of how to identify them and where to look.

The first topic to address is that there are plenty of them around, an idea central to this entire work. The Deadhead movement would make a very poor comparison to the early Christian community if its adherents were becoming scarce at this stage.

Though it is challenging to document with confidence, the evidence is that, with younger ones coming along every year, there are now more Deadheads than there have ever been.

RECENT ACTIVITY

One should not think of Deadheads as either the VW van driving drifters of past decades or just the graying ponytailed tape archivers of today. The crowds that have filled some of the country's largest stadiums for the recent summer tours of Dead and Company include a very substantial percentage who were of an age that meant they could not have become involved in this scene until long after Jerry Garcia's death. While the itinerants, the travelers who spend the summer getting to as many shows as possible, remain a very visible subset of the crowd, the young professionals who arrive at the show after a quick change into their tie-dye are just as much in evidence.

The size of the crowds at the Dead and Company summer tours is noteworthy but only in context. The summer of 2023 was notable for concert tours that reached mammoth proportions in terms of attendance and attention garnered in the popular press. Calculations of economic impact on the hosting cities of these huge shows became a common topic outside of the music world.

Press coverage of Dead and Company tended to be along the lines of "You'll never believe who is out touring again" and not about unprecedented ticket prices and revenue, as for other headline-making acts. The coverage did have a bit of a novel angle in that the band had billed this as their final tour. Interestingly, this heralded tour was taking place almost at the fiftieth anniversary of the first round of "last concerts" that the Grateful Dead did in 1974.

FIGURES ON THE SUMMER 2023 TOUR

The band themselves disclosed that the 2023 summer tour grossed a new high of $115 million in revenue and sold 845,000 tickets.

Such numbers sound remarkable by themselves when one considers the fact that it has been sixty years since the founding members of the Grateful Dead began performing together. Relative to the mega acts that are the hottest items in music today, these figures are maybe not so impressive but neither do the top-line totals tell the whole story.

The ticket brokerage service StubHub releases comparative information on demand for live concerts. Their data is segregated into several categories and genres of musical acts. One of those categories is "group acts," isolated from the iconic individual acts that dominated the celebrity news of that summer. Of the group acts, Coldplay led Stubhub's ranking as number one in the summer of 2023 while Dead and Company was second. Not bad for the seventh decade of concert performance.

The 845,000 tickets sold can be a guide for estimating the number of Deadheads, though a precise figure will never be easy to nail down. A first complication in relying on concert attendance figures is that a fair portion of senior Deadheads today take advantage of the excellent live streaming services now available to enjoy a "couch tour" from the comfort of their own homes. Out of those who do join the crowds at the concert venues, there is still more parsing to do. A substantial number will always be those who go to more than one concert on the tour. One the flip side, there are also significant numbers, especially in this year billed a final one, who are simply "Dead-curious," attending their first or second show but a long way from accepting the label Deadhead.

ESTIMATED POPULATION OF DEADHEADS

A rough figure of the total number of Deadheads, with generous upper and lower bounds, can be deduced by applying some assumptions and estimates to those different tour behaviors. By very rough estimates, the 845,000 number might first be reduced by 25 percent for the portion of the ticketed crowd that was only Dead-curious and not a Deadhead. Those who attended multiple shows will cause the ticket sales numbers to overestimate the population; thus a further 20 percent reduction might be a reasonable adjustment for those frequent flyers.

Determining a factor by which to inflate—to account for those who sat out the summer and did not contribute to tickets sales—is tricky in that it assumes that one has a starting understanding of what the true number of Deadheads is. If there were the same numbers of Deadheads that sat out all of the summer tour as went to multiple shows, those factors balance, and we're left with an estimate of total Deadheads somewhere north of 600,000.

Further round figures can be applied to estimate the degree of separation of any average adult from a Deadhead. If each of the, say, 650,000 Deadheads has 200 (nonoverlapping) active acquaintances, then half of the population of Americans ages 25–80 would have a Deadhead as an acquaintance. Those 125 million acquaintances are not, of course, evenly distributed, either demographically or geographically. If we consider just the demographic that has decided to look into this book, then one of the original premises of this work can be assumed to be demonstrated: virtually every adult book reader in America knows a Deadhead.

OTHER MEASURES OF SUCCESS

Historically, the bands with the highest total concert tour attendance and tour revenue are also, in general, the top acts for record sales. Neither of these measures were ones on which the Grateful Dead made much of an impact. With the exception of 1987, when the surprise hit "Touch of Grey" got top ten airplay, there were no occasions in their thirty-year performance career in which the band topped the standings for highest revenue touring groups. Of the all-time highest revenue rock tours, none of the top one hundred were by the Grateful Dead.

There is many a manner and method of ranking musical acts for total career record sales. No matter the varying factors that they include or estimate (stream, download, etc.), they all agree on the fact that the Grateful Dead are not a part of the lists of top sellers. Most readers will be able to guess which vastly popular "classic rock" and pop acts show up frequently in those charts. Which of those competing measures are most accurate is not important to the topic of this work. Those rankings are an important reference point, though, to understanding the significance of another measure of a band's enduring impact, and this measure is one that demonstrates how the Grateful Dead stand out from their contemporaries.

Another measure of a band's significance, apart from record sales and concert tour revenue, is how often the music is played by other musicians in live performance. This is a measure that demonstrates the longevity of the Grateful Dead but it also shows, in a striking way, how different they are from other groups of their time. What the data on frequency of live performance points out most clearly is something about the nature of the Deadheads, which is the proper subject of this work. The rich symbiosis created between the band and the crowd was always the magic ingredient that made the phenomenon unique. It bears repeating that there never would have been two thousand plus concerts over thirty years played by one band without an intensely devoted fan base coming back for more night after night.

A free wiki-like service, Setlist.fm, is an excellent source of data on the frequency of live musical performances. That site "considers a setlist to be the list of the songs a band or artist *actually played* during a concert," and music lovers use it to collect and share information on their favorite performers. The front page of the statistics section shows overall figures on the most covered artists, which details which bands' original songs have been performed by other performers ("covered").[1]

---

1. See Setlist.fm, "Most Covered Artists," https://www.setlist.fm/statistics.

Table 1. Ranking of Bands Most Often Covered by Other Performers

Setlist.fm	As of Nov. 2024
The Beatles	138,797
Pink Floyd	138,158
Grateful Dead	105,558
Traditional	104,828
Led Zeppelin	62,061
Bob Dylan	59,397
"Songs by the Beatles were covered 138,797 times."	

The figures shown are data on the top acts in terms of how often their songs are played by others. Most of the groups listed there will come as no surprise based on the total record sales over their careers. For the Grateful Dead to be on that list is an extreme outlier based on its lack of correlation with record sales totals. That alone marks them as a different sort of phenomenon, but the pattern by which they have been covered also reveals something about the ways they are unique.

INTERPRETING FIGURES ON COVERED SONGS

A few qualifiers are in order before drawing a too-sweeping set of conclusions from this data. The first is to take note of the top-selling acts that do not appear on this list. The bands that populate the top of this chart are generally those that had a heyday in past decades but who no longer tour under the original band name. If an act is still performing under the name that was on the record (Bruce Springsteen, Elton John, name-of-your-favorite-band-here), then their performances of their own songs are not covers and do not contribute to the number reported in the chart shown here. The covers measure indicates who *else* has played their songs.

The Rolling Stones are outliers here, as they are by most measures. They are near the top of the charts both for career record sales and for revenue on their monster tours, as are most others in the top ten of most covered bands. The Stones have the further distinction of a high rating for being covered by other bands even as they continue touring under their original name. This means they are not getting the "self-cover" credit that the Dead's surviving members get when they perform. In truth, this comes down to a matter of definition and artist preference. In their touring in the 2020s, Dead and Company and the Rolling Stones are essentially equal in the percentage of the original band members that are on stage. To honor Jerry Garcia's memory, the surviving band members decided after his passing that there would be no future performances under the name Grateful Dead, and so all of the performances by the many permutations of bands formed by the survivors are counted as covers.

The degree to which self-covers contribute to these statistics can be found by going a level deeper at Setlist.fm. The case of the Dead is not unique in having the original performers' self-covers contribute significantly to their totals. Paul McCartney is listed as the number one performer of Beatles covers, with fully two times the number of performances as the second most frequent. (To further illustrate the previous point, McCartney would not be counted as covering his own compositions from the post-Beatles time period.) Roger Waters is the number two performer of Pink Floyd covers, Robert Plant is the number two most frequent doing Led Zeppelin covers. Not to be outdone, Mick Jagger is listed as the sixth most frequent act to cover the Rolling Stones. The touring combination of Bob Dylan and Tom Petty is the number one contributor to Dylan's totals. While not related to the topic of self-covers, but rather as a measure of their connectedness, it is interesting that out of the top eight contributors for Dylan, four are Dead-related bands.

It should not be glossed over what an oddity it is that the Grateful Dead are so near the top in this listing of bands most covered by other acts. As stated, all of the others on the list consistently topped the charts for record sales. Their sales totals, according to several measures, are ten to twenty times greater than the totals of the Grateful Dead; maybe even as much as one hundred times greater in the case of the Beatles. Digging a little deeper, to see how these anomalous totals on covers came about, reveals a little more about what makes the band, and really, the fan base, different.

DIFFERENT PATTERNS OF COVER FOR DIFFERENT BANDS

The distinction between the pattern of bands covering Beatles songs as opposed to Grateful Dead songs might be characterized as wide versus deep. Everybody loves Beatles songs, and many, many acts will perform one or two of their numbers. On the other hand, not everybody loves Grateful Dead songs, but the bands that play them tend to play a night of *all* Grateful Dead songs, which is just what their fans want to hear. Their different math might be characterized this way:

- Beatles = 10,000,000 fans x 20 songs x 2 listens per year = a total of 400 million listens

- GD = 100,000 fans x 40 songs x 100 listens per year = a total of 400 million listens

The helpful people at Setlist.fm have provided some additional data on the differences in the pattern of musical acts that cover Beatles and Grateful Dead songs. The Beatles total number of covers is 30 percent higher, but they were generated by 600 percent more acts that did the performing (5,400 for the Beatles and 870 for the Grateful Dead). This makes for a very different average number of songs covered for the two groups by each act: twenty-three covers per act for the Beatles and one hundred and three performances of Grateful Dead songs per act.

The frequency at which the twenty top covering acts play covers is remarkably similar for the two groups. The total covers played by the top twenty for each group are 56,200 for the Beatles and 63,900 for the Grateful Dead. That they should even be in the same ballpark, much less a higher number for the Dead, is stunning given their different degree of mass appeal. The real difference between them is found in the long, long tail of five thousand performers who play Beatles songs: the top twenty acts for the Beatles represent only 45 percent of all of the Beatles covers, while the top twenty acts account for 70 percent of the Grateful Dead covers. By these measures, of how frequently the fans go out to see a live performance of music that originated with these bands, the Deadheads' affection for their favorite music is a match even for the appeal of the Beatles.

TRIBUTE V. COVER BANDS

Before leaving this topic (which has strayed a bit from comparisons to the early Jesus movement), it is worth offering a few comments on the differences that might be noted between a tribute band, a cover band, and a band or artist that does a cover of a song. It is not unreasonable to think that any band or individual performer of popular musical today would be able to do a Beatles or Dylan song if asked. These are part of a common canon of music that has permeated our culture. Tribute bands, at their extreme, commit themselves to reproducing the stage performance of a single act. Beatlemania might be thought of as the archetype: in their look and sound, they try to reproduce the original performance as nearly as they can, and that is what the fans pay to see. There are very successful tribute bands for nearly all prominent acts, and these contribute significantly to cover totals for those groups.

The relatively high totals for covers of Grateful Dead songs is the result of a large number of bands that stick to playing strictly, or nearly so, only Grateful Dead music. That approach, though, does not really fit the pattern of tribute bands. The distinction is in the style of performance. There never was much to see at a Dead show: no costumes, no stage antics, no props. As far as trying to sound like the band, there never was a single sound to copy, because the band never played a song the same way twice. The appeal for Dead fans was never in hearing a performance that was "just like the record," whereas that is the special attraction for fans of tribute bands.

What Dead fans still turn out to see, or hear, really, is a band that can do live improvisation in the context of beloved songs. There are several groups, Dark Star Orchestra notable among them, that have had great success in bringing Deadheads out to hear a night of live Grateful Dead music; DSO, as that group is known, has now performed more concerts of Grateful Dead music than the original band did. One website that lists Grateful Dead cover bands has more than eight hundred entries. Even in an age when every fan could sit home and listen to any one of hundreds of finely recorded live performances by the original band, a respectable number will venture out to hear the magic happen again. What the Deadheads seek, perpetually, is to once again feel that communal spirit recommended in Scripture where it is written ". . . look for how to prod one another to love and good deeds, not giving up getting together amongst yourselves, as is the custom of some, but encouraging one another" (Hebrews 10:24-25).

The Deadhead trait: Deadheads value new experiences over new possessions.

The comment: This is by no means a characteristic that is peculiar to Deadheads. Any large fan base with shared opinions about what is most important in life can be expected to have common attitudes about the value of material possessions. Looking for evidence of conspicuous consumption is one approach to evaluating how the Deadhead crowd falls on this spectrum. A visit to the parking lot scene before a Dead event will prove the point: there are many coveted objects on display and being purchased, but these things are coveted because of what they say about the buyer's devotion to the band, not because they convey status. In this the crowd conforms to an early Christian ideal; it is written, "Are any of you wise and understanding? Show that your actions are good with a humble lifestyle that comes from wisdom" (Jas 3:13).

3

Baseball and Deadheads

The passage: "Whoever is not against us if for us . . ." (Mark 9:40).

The context: Of all of the passages used to introduce chapters in this work, this is the only one that quotes Jesus. His words are attached to a story that suggest a time when the religious expression by his followers was not dictated by authorities (also discussed in ch. 1). The disciples had brought reports that there were others out and about in Galilee using Jesus' name in healing, and they wanted them shut down. Jesus declined to put boundaries on expressions of faith in his name (in Mark's narrative this comes just after Jesus brings a child into the company of the disputing disciples to illustrate a lesson in how to discern who is "for us").

✝

Half of all of the teams in major league baseball have held Grateful Dead tribute nights in recent years. At those ballgames, fans receive commemorative T-shirts, are entertained by cover bands before the game begins, and all of the diversions presented between innings incorporate the theme of the evening. That the sport that has been the image of continuity in America would embrace the band that was once the poster children of the rebellious '60s shows just how much the reputation of the Grateful Dead has changed. In this light, the point made in the Introduction, regarding the Federal Reserve chairman's attendance at Dead shows over a fifty-year time span, is recognized as an exemplar, not an outlier. Are the Grateful Dead now on track to join Mom and apple pie as symbols of all that is good about the US of A?

WHY BASEBALL TEAMS HOLD GRATEFUL DEAD NIGHTS

Several facts about the Deadhead phenomenon become evident when we see this subpopulation, with its proudly countercultural origins, now sharing events with a sphere of society that is at the very center of the American identity. The first is that the promoters of the events at the ballgames see a target population large enough that appealing to it can meaningfully increase the crowd that turns out that night. It is again worth pointing out the enduring nature of the phenomenon if a crowd of significant size can be targeted even after several decades have passed since the band was last active.

The organizers of Grateful Dead nights at ballgames must believe other things about Deadheads as well, besides that there are a significant number of them around. They first must have confidence that the "normal" patrons of the ballpark will not react negatively to seeing a crowd of Deadheads show up. This should not be a difficult proposition to accept by this time after so many other teams have had successful events (and some teams have done it more than once). On the flip side, for the teams to go out and appeal to the Deadheads, the promoters would also have to believe that they would be interested in showing up and that they will enjoy being at a baseball game.

Promoters with a good understanding of the mindset both of baseball fans and of Deadheads would see a natural overlap between them. Those who understand them would further expect that the Deadheads who do show up for the tribute night are not making their first trip to the ballpark. The common tastes of baseball fans and Deadheads might be revealed in common criticisms that nonfans make of each: their events take too long, and there is too much time when nothing is happening.

WHY GRATEFUL DEAD FANS LIKE BASEBALL

The game of baseball has this shared attribute with Grateful Dead shows: there is a complexity that unfolds at a deliberate pace. This is not to say that there is not excitement all along the way. A home run can happen in the first inning, even with the first batter, and a concert can open with something sublime. The most prized feature at each event, though, are those exquisite treasures toward the end, which are built up from what came earlier: the slow revealing of a pitcher's strategy to navigate his way several times through a lineup of sluggers and the gradual flowering of a jam sequence that references songs played earlier in the show.

The criticism that baseball games and Dead shows take too long suggests that the fans of each share a trait: being patient as the event they are enjoying reaches its resolution. Because baseball is the only major team sport that is not time bound, the game only ends when a set of conditions are met, not when the clock (and the fans' attention span) has expired. All sporting events have the element of the unknown as part of their appeal (unlike, for instance, classic drama or opera, where the outcome is not in doubt). Because the ending of a baseball game is rule based, it has the added feature that at single unique junctures—in the ninth inning or later—there is uncertainty whether the game will end in that moment or not, let alone in whose favor; the game could end in favor of team *A* or team *B*, or not at all, being left unresolved until more innings of play decide the matter. The only comparable situation in team sports is the rare circumstance in the last seconds of a basketball game in which scoring two points, three points, or none at all can produce three different outcomes.

That there is ambiguity in the possible outcome of a Grateful Dead song, as there is in a ninth inning, is welcome and appreciated.

This is true even in the case of one's favorite song—in fact, probably more so. The song may transition off to another song after just the first verse, or perhaps after the second. The favorite song may be arrived at by a meandering path, without any of its lyrics having been sung, before the way is made back along that path to the first song or again further into a third, unexpected song, one with which it has never been paired. Deadheads and baseball fans savor the manifold alternative outcomes. The patient approach to the enjoyment of musical and sporting events fits into an approach to life in general that comports with advice given to early Christians; it is written, "Be quick to listen, slow to speak, slow to anger" (Jas 1:19).

HOW COMMON INTERESTS ARE MANIFEST

Common interests in sporting and musical entertainment should be expected to manifest in more activities than just showing up at the stadium on certain nights. As much as baseball fans can revel in reviewing the fine points of a game and develop new analytic metrics, so Deadheads can obsess about patterns of song performance. Anyone who is familiar with both behaviors would not dismiss the common attributes of a fan's checking a box score the day after a game with someone making a careful review of the setlist from a recent concert.

For some fans, interest in the sequence of songs for one concert is just the starting point. What is the likelihood that certain songs will be played on the same night? Were they played sequentially or separated from one another by other songs (in whole or part)? Were any songs brought back after years of not being performed? Were any themes evident, in songs with similar lyrics or in their reference to locations? All of this goes into a full appreciation of a concert.

So it is also with baseball: any casual fan can be thrilled by a home run that wins a game. The fan who knows that Ozzie Smith had never in his career hit a home run while batting left-handed will be that much more thrilled when he wins a playoff game by doing that for the first time. As much as the internet now allows avid baseball fans to pore over every detail of every past game, and aggregate results over many years, so Deadheads can analyze every combination of song sequences for their frequency and pattern.

At one step removed from the analysis of single events, there is a common realm of the aggregated baseball season as a whole and the concert tour as an entity. Other sports have seasons of course, but the baseball season is particularly extended. When the final weeks of September roll around, teams play crucial games against teams that they already played many times over the course of the six-month season. Each turn at bat is then heightened by the player's knowledge of the outcome of each previous encounter with the opposing pitcher. Those one-on-one episodes embedded in a team game are unique to baseball.

A comparable kind of accumulated interest builds as a concert tour unfolds. For most rock acts this is not the case, as each night's show is just like all the others on the tour. Because each Dead show is unique, as the last few shows of a tour are on the horizon, interest grows in how it will all play out: which songs are due to be played, which have likely been played for the last time, and which will be played in different combinations than was the case way back when the tour began.

Throughout this work comparisons will be made about attributes that Deadheads share with other populations. In each case no claim is made that there is a strict one-to-one exclusive correspondence. Much of what has been said about appreciating the ambiguity of the progress of a baseball game with a Dead show could be said just as well about fans of jazz music. Perhaps it is not a coincidence that jazz and baseball had overlapping decades of dominating American culture. Just as it is true that fans of other music make good baseball fans, so it is that baseball cannot be said to be the only sport of interest for Deadheads. Evidence that there are many Deadheads who are very passionate hockey fans can be found in the fact that several hockey teams have also held Grateful Dead nights. Perhaps in counterpoint to the patience described above, it is the quick reversal and the unexpected turn that fans of hockey and jam bands both appreciate.

THE PRIME MOVER

The frequent events targeted to Deadheads by major (and minor) league baseball is not solely due to well-researched insight into the broader interests of their fan base. In truth, it is unlikely that any such events would have taken place but for the fact that the Grateful Dead charitable arm, the Rex Foundation, played an active role as a fundraising organization.

The Rex foundation was begun in 1983 in memory of one of the Grateful Dead road crew, Donald "Rex" Jackson. The term "roadies" would never do justice to the commitment displayed by those that did so much to move the band and its more-than-average load of gear from place to place on the unending tours. At the time of his unfortunate death, the band organized their many charitable donation activities into an entity that bore his name. These days when baseball and hockey teams hold Grateful Dead nights, with commemorative T-shirts and theme tickets, the Rex Foundation is the beneficiary. That the broader Grateful Dead organization has had, as an integral part, a long-standing charitable arm may come as a surprise to casual observers, but it is an additional fact that should create a positive impression in the minds of Christians.

$$\mathcal{T}$$

The Deadhead trait: Deadheads are always eager to make the acquaintance of other Deadheads.

The comment: Two Deadheads who have just learned of their mutual interest very quickly find that they have a lot to talk about. This is true whether they have just met for the first time or have known each other for some time and never got around to the topic of their favorite band. They are in a way like members of a common nationality who discover each other while living in a foreign land: whatever their differences, they revel while they can in sharing something very important to them that they have in common. When a crowd of Deadheads is gathered, they are no longer strangers to one another. Each knows a good deal about the others, without knowing any specifics. They operate on the assumption that was expressed by Congressman Nickel, quoted in the Introduction, and proven reliable over and over, that Deadheads can be counted on to be likable. In their interactions with one another Deadheads seem to have taken to heart the advice of the apostle Paul for how the early members of the Jesus movement should behave toward one another: "Show sincere love; abhor evil, cling to what is good. Hold one another in brotherly love; take the lead in honoring one another" (Rom 12:9–10).

4

Uniqueness of Deadheads as Fans

The passage: "Many followed him, but scattered when he died . . ." (Acts 5:37).

The context: The comment in this passage comes from a council meeting that was held to decide how to deal with apostles who would not stop spreading the word about Jesus. Despite being jailed and ordered to stop preaching, the apostles persisted. A wise member of the council, the same Gamaliel quoted in chapter 1, reminds the others that they have watched several flash-in-the-pan leaders of the masses come and go. In each previous case, once the leader was gone, the crowds quickly faded away. He advises the council to simply observe the Jesus movement to see if it, too, would dissipate in due time, as the others had.

✝

Many a pop phenomenon has come and gone in the time since the Grateful Dead first started drawing crowds. A modern-day Gamaliel might take note of the range of acts that had a larger fan base than that of the Grateful Dead, with record sales many times higher, but which nevertheless have not stood the test of time. As the ancient Gamaliel took an evidence-based approach to evaluating the Jesus movement, his modern counterpart might consider the signs of longevity in the Deadhead phenomenon as indicators of something unique going on. The question to explore now is whether those unique characteristics will produce a special kind of longevity, one that is not merely of human origin.

THE MAJOR MILESTONE

As the Deadhead movement passes through successive milestones of longevity, it further distinguishes itself from the type of fan loyalty that other artists have enjoyed. Other musical acts have certainly had an intensely loyal fan following, though few are so robust as to have earned a label as well-recognized as "Deadhead." Even fewer, though, are the fan followings that have passed a milestone as significant as the death of Jerry Garcia. Only after fully three decades have elapsed since the passing of, say, Jimmy Buffet, would the appropriate time come to evaluate the lasting power of his fan base as compared to the Deadheads.

The continued flourishing of the Deadhead movement three decades after the death of Jerry Garcia, as has been detailed in previous chapters, will likely come as a surprise to those who mistook the movement as a cult of personality. Certainly, a large measure of hero reverence did attach to Jerry throughout his performing career, similar to the kind directed to Jim Morrison and other contemporaries. Even today, the Jerry iconography is very much in evidence, and for sale in every conceivable format, at Dead and Company and Dead-related events.

The true appeal of the Grateful Dead, though, was always about much more than the intriguing personality of one individual. The goal that the band set for themselves, and doggedly pursued, was the greater potential that was to be found in the collaboration of all the members together. Somewhat unique among the big rock bands of their time, they sought to make *new* music every night, and this required the participation of each member. The success and enduring appeal of the band was based on that collaboration, in many ways the opposite of just a star performer with a backing ensemble. Based on the record of success of Dead and Company and the many, many other bands playing Dead music today, there is every reason to expect that the phenomenon will not only outlive Jerry Garcia but each of the original band members as well.

A DEFINING CHARACTERISTIC

The nature of the Deadhead phenomenon has always been a bit unique. From very early on, the behavior of Deadheads has been chronicled as being different from the ordinary sort of rabid fan base enjoyed by many contemporary acts, though those other fan groups were generally larger. What set the Deadheads apart, and earned them recognition as a kind of subspecies with their own name, was their devotion to the music of one band almost to the exclusion of all others. (A case study of one individual's obsession with the music is documented in ch. 6.) Deadheads generally listen to many styles of music, but as a distinguishing feature from fans of other bands, a much higher percentage of the music they listen to comes from a single band.

Further evidence of the Deadheads' perpetual readiness to consume ever more Grateful Dead music can be found back in the traditional realm of sales of recorded music. The forty-ninth release in the series of archived live recordings (now termed Dave's Picks), hit the Billboard charts on February 10, 2024, at number twenty-five. The reliable pattern of consumption by devoted Deadheads allows them to sell just enough copies with each release, all booked in the same week, to break the threshold for the charts. This put them once again in the unfamiliar company of music industry giants that they would not normally be mentioned in the same breath with. With that accomplishment, they became the musical act with the most top-forty-charting albums in the sixty-eight-year history of the Billboard 200.

Table 2. Ranking of Performers with the Most Top-Forty-Charting Albums
on the Billboard 200

Grateful Dead	59
Elvis Presley	58
Frank Sinatra	58
Barbra Streisand	54
Bob Dylan	51
The Rolling Stones	48

BEYOND THE LIVE CONCERT

The success of the distribution of archived concerts points to another kind of transcendence that bodes well for the longevity of the movement. As much as each round of a stadium-packing tour shows that the movement can transcend the personality of Garcia, it still takes place in the same setting as the original phenomenon: the thrilling sensory experience of a live rock concert. The steady consumption of concerts in recorded format, however, shows that even when they are in an entirely different setting, at home on their couch, Deadheads still have an unquenchable appetite for the music and always for new versions of the songs that they know so well.

The Deadheads' signature behavior of always seeking more music from a single band could not persist were it not for the band's unique attribute of producing so much material. Call it symbiosis, call it coevolution, or just call it the unique phenomenon that it is, the appetite of Deadheads for new musical adventures at each concert happily coincided with the band's wish to always live at the edge of new inspiration. This enabled the original trademark feature of the Deadheads of traveling to as many shows as possible, as well as perpetuating the movement through the recording of those two thousand plus unique concerts and distributing copies of these recordings. These traits are detailed in subsequent chapters.

So, in the beginning, there was the Grateful Dead's unique approach to performance; this was supported by the unique willingness of Deadheads to travel the country to see multiple concerts. Today we see the unique aspect of the Dead phenomenon having a currency that is entirely out of proportion to what would be expected of other aging rock originals. Just as remarkable, but left unquantifiable, is the unique degree of coherence that distinguishes the Deadhead community. But does this all add up to an ultimate uniqueness, the kind that produces a phenomenon that far outlasts the generation of all the original participants? The kind of longevity that Gamaliel, with remarkable foresight, hinted was possible?

BEYOND THE DEADHEADS

To say that the Deadhead phenomenon has unique features and therefore that the music will live on in future generations does not imply that it will be the *only* music from this time that will survive. Artistic movements that have stood the test of time were never constituted of a single individual. Where great art is made, there are many simultaneous practitioners. And separate from their peer group of the "classic rock" acts of the '60s and '70s, there are in addition a cohort of jam bands today whose performance style and fan devotion are consistent with the Dead style.

The fans of other jam bands are a subject that has to be considered when evaluating, in the first place, whether the number of Deadheads is increasing today and, in the second place, whether it can be expected to continue to do so. The jam bands sprang up to fill the vacuum left by the end of the Grateful Dead touring. They met the appetite of many fans for the same thing that was sought at the Dead shows: musicians going on stage with the intent to improvise new music in front of a live audience.

Just as we would say that what was sought by '80s and '90s Deadheads was not much different from what was sought by '60s and '70s Deadheads, so it should not be much more of a stretch to recognize that what the jam bands' fans are seeking corresponds with what the Deadheads were after. If it is just the name of the band that has changed while the aesthetic pursuit is the same, then there may be need for a broadened definition of the Deadhead movement. There are many participants in the current Dead scene who, to external appearances, would have been considered Dead-heads in previous decades and yet who do not take that name for themselves. Of course, the only true identifier of a Deadhead is someone who calls themself that. There is today a cohort of fans who attend as many shows as do the Deadheads but, because their affinity is not solely for the Dead, do not identify as Deadheads. They can, and do, go to see a variety of bands for the same live music experience they get with the Dead.

If future generations are still discussing this movement, the distinction between Deadheads and the fans of the broader jam-band genre (are they Jam-hearts?) might resemble the questions of definition that were prominent in the early decades of the Jesus movement. The earliest followers of Jesus were essentially all Jews. As the movement spread and grew in later decades, more and more of the believers were not Jews. The hotly debated question at that time became whether one needed to become a Jew first to be a true follower of Jesus. Ultimately the movement could not be contained and the term Christian was applied to all believers, without regard to origins. There may be a similar outcome if this current movement persists long into the future: what started out originally as just Deadheads could eventually evolve into some-thing of broader scope.

CHILDREN OF DEADHEADS

The special case of the children of Deadheads deserves some con-sideration. (A further testament to the uniqueness of the phenom-enon is that this should even be a noteworthy topic; for how many other fan groups is the commitment so significant that the impact on children is meaningful?) These poor dears have listened to endless recordings of studio albums and concerts and likely been dragged along to more shows than would have been their pref-erence. It has always been so. The back cover of the band's third album is a group photo that includes several people of tender years who were regarded as an essential part of the scene.

Not all parents brought their kids along to the concerts, but the common Deadhead characteristic of constantly listening to one style of music is cliché enough that there is a well-traveled joke about it. A family is driving along somewhere and a whiny vice comes from the back seat pleading, "Mom, do we have to listen to the Grateful Dead *all* the time?" The mother calmly pulls the car over to the side of the road, safely brings it to a stop, turns to face the children and says, "Bobby, Jerry, get out."

Parents toting multiple children to shows has long been accepted behavior and lives on, abundantly so, in the Dead and Company era, but what are the attitudes of those kids when they are free to make their own choices? There are now many thousands of young adults who were brought along to concerts in their youth and were thus exposed to music and behavior that was not in the mainstream.

A very unscientific sample of friends, relations, and people met at concerts has found that those raised by Deadheads are favorably disposed to the music, like it well enough (and their parents as well), but they are unlikely to call themselves Deadheads. That is a term that, in their minds, applies to the previous generation, not to them. Very much like those who came to the jam-band scene of their own accord, the children of Deadheads might be found attending as many Dead-related concerts as one who proudly claims the identity, yet they insist it is not for them. Time will tell; perhaps there will come a time when it is a common expression to say, "I was raised as a Deadhead but stopped attending concerts."

☉

The Deadhead trait: No one stops being a Deadhead.

The comment: This is not to say that there are not lapsed Deadheads (leaving aside the definition problem: how can one say that a person has ceased to be a Deadhead without a standard to judge by?). It is not uncommon that a Deadhead's frequency of listening to recorded Dead music or attending live performances may wax and wane over the years. The same might be said about baseball fans. Disenchantment with the fortunes of a favorite team, or changes in how fortunes are being made, or with the style of the game are to be expected. But when a thrilling pennant race captures their fancy, and teams with compelling characters again catch a fan's attention, they will recall those facets of the game that they always loved. So it is with Deadheads: the purchase on one's soul that can occur, as described in chapter 6, does not simply disappear. Seasons of disenchantment may last for years and decades, but the affection for what made one first become a Deadhead remains. People do not reverse and suddenly *not* like the songs they once loved. What has been so remarkable about the universe of Dead cover bands is that so many fans are being brought back in to rediscover that which had taken hold of them at that "deeper level." It abides and is ready to blossom when that same sweet sound is heard again. The advice given by the apostle Paul to early believers is relevant here; it is written, "Examine everything carefully and hang on to what is good" (1 Thess 5:21); and again, "Whatever is true, honorable, just, pure, pleasing, commendable, if there is any excellence and anything worthy of praise, think about these things" (Phil 4:8).

5

The New Now

The passage: "The Spirit fell on them as it had on us at the beginning . . ." (Acts 11:15).

The context: This passage recounts an occasion when the apostle Peter was first preaching to a group that was outside of Jewish society. Up until that point, Jews had made up the whole of the Jesus movement. Peter recognized that the same sense of conversion that the original believers had experienced was now taking place in a new setting. In this circumstance, from inside the movement, God's action can be recognized with certainty. This can be contrasted with the passages attached to chapter 1 and chapter 4 in which outside observers struggled to recognize divine action at work in the world.

†

The previous chapter detailed the unique approach taken by the Grateful Dead in prioritizing improvisation in the performance of live music. The contrast of this approach to that of other rock bands' emphasis on studio recordings was analogized by Jerry Garcia as being like the difference between building a ship in a bottle and taking a rowboat out on the ocean.[1] Whatever he saw as the merits of going to sea in a rowboat, it was this approach that consistently turned out crowds to see what would happen.

GRATEFUL DEAD AND IMPRESSIONISM

An analogy more related to art may prove helpful in understanding the appetite of Deadheads to return, over and over, to witnessing the adventure in the rowboat. When the art movement that came to be called Impressionism was new, it stood in stark contrast to the standard, mainline school of painting of the time. The Academic approach to painting valued the most life-like possible representations that could be made on canvas (in the days before photography was commonly available). These paintings might be likened to the most highly polished of studio recordings, with each instrument so delicately and precisely rendered that fans would forevermore only wish to hear the song played exactly as it had been recorded.

The imperative for the new style of painting was to complete a work quickly enough to capture the fleeting essence of a moment, usually working out in the elements. The goal was to present just an impression, not create a reproduction. Transmitting a sense of immediacy to the viewer, a sense of what it felt like to be there at that moment, took precedence over getting the shape of each leaf just exactly perfect. Performing live improvised music has the same artistic ambition; maybe every vocal is not pitched exactly right, and one instrument did not come in on the beat as it should have, but the audience and performers have a shared sense of *now*. Everyone heard a new musical creation take shape at the same moment.

A Deadhead's desire to always want to hear yet another version of "Scarlet Begonias" might be more understandable if it is compared to the Monet fan's interest in viewing yet another of

1. Garcia, "Complete Interview," 17:40.

his renderings of water lilies. Each finished piece is different, and each new one that is encountered adds a depth of understanding to all those that have been previously appreciated. Curiously, though, the way we enjoy these works today could never have been contemplated by the artists at the time that they were being created. The painters, of course, always intended to leave behind a permanent record, but would not have imagined that anyone, even someone with only the most casual level of interest, would be able to compare all the artist's works side by side on a desktop display.

LEAVING A RECORD (NOT RECORDS)

While each live Dead event was meant to be experienced by a crowd of people sharing a specific place and time, there were recordings being made for a later hearing. Originally, the recording was just for the band to review and only subsequently were made with the plan that they be released on vinyl as better versions of the music than was being captured in the studio. In time, audience members made their own recordings at concerts, wishing to make it possible to revisit those fleeting, transcendent moments. The lengths that independent fans went to in order to initially record the shows, and then to reproduce, trade, and spread their tapes, is all the stuff of legend. With technological advances, these early efforts at dissemination of the live shows would soon seem like little puttering propeller planes compared to the jumbo-jet age that was on the horizon.

Earlier chapters provided facts and figures on the steady consumption by Deadheads, via live events and issues of CD recordings, of new musical experiences. All of this is dwarfed by what has been wrought by the union of Deadhead obsessiveness with access to the newfangled internet's treasure trove of recorded concerts. Not unlike the ability of baseball fans today to use data searches to determine the frequency of an all left-handed infield turning a double play on all left-handed runners during the third inning on a Wednesday, the vast power of the information age is a boon to Deadheads who wish to search for every possible song combination that might have been played. More than that, the interested party can get access to each of those shows and explore for themselves how the transition between certain songs was accomplished in different years.

BRINGING IT ALL TOGETHER

The Internet Archive is the principal (but not only) repository that allows Deadheads to track down virtually any Dead-related concert and song that was recorded. Amidst the millions upon millions of stored books, images, archived web pages, copies of software, films and TV shows on the Internet Archive, there are seventeen thousand items in the Grateful Dead collection. These concert recordings, with multiple uploads of many shows by different people who were there, make up just a portion of the 260,000 items in the Live Music Archive on that site, but the Grateful Dead recordings are among the items most often accessed. Figures posted on Internet Archive show that there have been more than two hundred million views of, or visits to, the Grateful Dead Archive, making up the bulk of the views of the music section. As was the case in the discussion of ticket sales and covered songs, the presentation of these numbers is not to try to prove that the Grateful Dead is the most popular thing on the internet (the collection of Islamic sermons has 297 million views). It is just presented as a further data point to show that the Grateful Dead has a currency that would surprise anyone who dismissed them as a relic of a bygone era.

The question of *why* there have been two hundred million occasions of someone going to an archived version of a Grateful Dead concert relates directly to the phenomenon of their longevity. What were fans seeking who went to show after show on a single tour? What are fans seeking who go out to see the cover bands that are active across the land? What are the serial buyers of CD releases seeking? To again experience the moment of exhilaration when familiar music sounds new and novel music seems to be familiar. Each occasion of hearing a version of a song that has not been heard before can refresh the same sensation of your most enjoyable moment of listening to music. Deadheads return to the font over and over because of their faith, which has been validated time and again, that they know they can experience the same "*now*-ness" of when the music was performed for the first time.

BE THERE NOW

One key role that the archive plays is in allowing any interested person to go back in time and experience a pivotal moment they themselves had experienced at a Grateful Dead concert. When the original event was taking place, bounded in time and space, a number of factors could contribute to a person's appreciation of the show. It was a common circumstance that a person would come out of a show with a new understanding of that common phrase from the earliest days, that "There is *nothing* like a Grateful Dead concert." As decades roll on and lifestyles change, the question might arise as to how much of that sensation was the music itself and how much was due to the circumstances. The Archive allows each person to investigate that question for themselves. Given the volume of visits that are made to the site, it would appear that those who make that return visit get a positive answer as to whether it is possible to revisit that musical moment and feel the magic once more. Doing so demonstrates another milestone of the viability of the ongoing movement: it now transcends time, in addition to the absence of Garcia and the concert venue as a listening environment.

Accessing the Internet Archive to listen to Dead music has a further distinction from relying on cover bands and CD releases: it is absolutely and completely *free*. Listening to any number of songs from any number of concerts for any amount of time requires only the effort to search for them. This is a resource with great potential for making new Deadheads. There is plenty of advice on what to listen to among the three hundred thousand comments that have been posted along with the recordings in the Grateful Dead forum of the Internet Archive.

THE NEW WAY

The efficacy of this approach to becoming a Deadhead, through access to past recordings only, without ever having experienced the first round of concerts thirty to sixty years ago, is today fueling the movement. After a certain number of positive experiences, the listener knows in their heart that delving into yet another highly recommended show can result in the familiar exalted state.

The validity of the experience of the next generation Deadheads, those who missed the first round of shows, brings to mind the Gospel writers' accounts of the spread of faith. In one of the most familiar of stories from John's Gospel, doubting Thomas is told by the risen Jesus that the fortunate ones are those who believe though they have not seen for themselves (John 20:29). This Gospel was written at a time when the number of those who had seen the events in Galilee for themselves was dwindling, and yet the movement continued to grow without bounds. It is a reasonable bet that nearly all of those who read the first edition of John's Gospel were among those that believed though they had not seen. (Incidentally, the Greek word rendered here as "fortunate," *makarioi*, is the same word that is familiar to Christians from the Beatitudes, where it is commonly translated as "happy" or "blessed." This is one of only two times that this particular Greek word is used in John's Gospel, and it comes in the last line before the sign-off. The only other use is in reference to those who put their faith into action [13:17]).

One notable case study of just this sort of second-generation conversion, by one who did not see the original band, is documented in the next chapter.

The trait: Deadheads love to hear new versions of their favorite songs.

The comment: Is it novelty that the Deadheads seek, or sameness? Yes. What is desired is a familiar sense of novelty produced by a common musical approach, over and over. In this pattern of consumption Deadheads are not unlike others who are passionate about other forms of great music. How many different performances of the same opera would a real fan like to hear? As many different versions as there are that can reproduce the sensation of hearing it all new once again.

In their confidence that they know a sure path to an enlightened state, Deadheads might join with those early Christians who understood "wisdom from above that is first pure, peaceful, gentle, yielding, filled with mercy and good actions, fair, and sincere" (Jas 3:17).

6

A Conversion Story

The passage: "Last of all, as one untimely born . . ." (1 Cor 15:8).

The context: The conversion story of the apostle Paul—he was knocked off his horse while on the road to Damascus—is one that is familiar to most Christians. It is recounted three times in the book of Acts, with some intriguing differences between the versions. One is presented in a narrative style (ch. 9), and two are presented as speeches by Paul, as he recalls past events (chs. 22 and 26). Curiously, none of the story elements that we find in Acts appear in any of the surviving letters written by Paul. The quote that is used to introduce this chapter is one of the few instances in which he references the transformation that took him from being hostile to the Jesus movement to being one of its greatest advocates. The common element between what Paul wrote and the tale as it is told in Acts is that he never saw Jesus in the flesh and yet saw the light.

✝

Every Deadhead can recount, in detail, the circumstances in which they felt themselves becoming a Deadhead. The stories are as varied as the population, though there are recurring themes in all these tales. Of all those accounts, one particular individual's story is worth recounting here, and for two reasons: the first is because it has significance for the further development of this movement; and the second, because it has striking parallels to significant events in the history of early Christianity.

John Mayer gave several press interviews in which he eloquently repeated his account of becoming a Deadhead. His depth of expression about the meaning of the music would be significant in itself but becomes multiplied in importance by the role he has taken on as one of the great evangelizers for the movement. In this context, the accounts of his conversion cannot help but remind Christians of the experience of the apostle Paul.

Consider: a person who never met the founder of the movement in the flesh, suddenly, in later life and as a public person, is dramatically reoriented to a new understanding of a movement that he previously misjudged. After a period of intense study, he becomes one of the greatest popularizers of the movement. Through his profound interpretation and exposition of the founder's work, he stimulates new growth in the movement by bringing it to audiences that had not previously been exposed to its power. Though his conversion took place unguided and in isolation, in time he became a close collaborator with the original cadre of the movement.

JOHN MAYER'S DESCRIPTION(S) OF HIS CONVERSION

Just as Scripture provides us with several accounts of Paul's dramatic encounter on the road to Damascus, which are harmonious, if not agreeing in every detail, so there are several versions of the modern conversion. The comments made by John Mayer on separate occasions about becoming a Deadhead do not contradict one another, but each telling provides some additional fine details that others do not. The vividness of the recollections, taken together, give an idea of how precisely the moment was impressed on his memory.

Mayer's published accounts all agree on which song he heard that knocked him off his horse: "Then 'Althea' came on, and everything just seemed to stop. I went, 'What is that?'"[1]

And again: "A [Pandora] station that wasn't far genetically from the Dead played 'Althea' and I heard this riff and went, 'What's that?' I actually came in from being outside in the pool, I was dripping wet and had to see what was on the iPod."[2]

And: "It was probably around 2011 when I first got into the music, based on a groove thing—the way the guitar was bouncing around on 'Althea.'"[3] Further detail and a bit of what caught the musician's ear: "'Althea' came on, and I was in Palm Springs . . . and I had never heard anybody do that and I couldn't—and it's a very rare thing before I heard Jerry Garcia playing the guitar; I couldn't tell what he was doing."[4]

More on what was different about this song: "As a guitar player, I had managed to burrow pretty deep into all the things that can happen on a guitar neck. . . . If I'm falling asleep and listening to music, I can watch the fretboard and map it. But I listened to this, and it was like I had never played an instrument."[5]

From there began the period of intense study. In 2013, years before there was any notion of performing with Bob Weir, he told Rolling Stone, "I've been listening to stuff and just falling in love with certain things. I've been listening to the Grateful Dead nonstop. Mark my words, the Grateful Dead are gonna make a comeback."[6]

The intensity of his absorption, common to all Deadheads, was unashamedly proclaimed several times: "I remember

1. Budnick, "Dead and Company Origin," para. 3.
2. Halperin, "Mayer Talks Grateful Dead," para. 2.
3. Fricke, "Mayer Playing with Dead and Company," para. 12.
4. Delray, "Mayer/Part 1," 1:13:30.
5. Budnick, "Dead and Company Origin," para. 3.
6. Doyle, "Mayer on His New Voice," para. 15.

downloading every Dick's Picks from iTunes. It's actually the only [music] on my iPhone, everything else is on the cloud."[7] "The topic of Grateful Dead music for me at that time was like, I want nothing but to think about it, talk about [it]—so I knew that it had taken some deeper sort of purchase inside of me on a deeper level than anything ever had."[8] Spoken like a true convert.

In the summer of 2023, his statements make clear that his enthusiasm had not dimmed, very much in keeping with other Deadheads. He also has an intriguing way of describing how it is that Deadheads can have a variety of interests and at the same time have a particular devotion to the music of one band: "I listen to this music every day. . . . Grateful Dead music has a whole extra dimension for me than listening to music. There's books, movies, theater, music, art, comedy, Grateful Dead. It's a completely different lobe of my brain than music."[9]

In keeping with the discussion in chapter 5 on the importance of the electronic resources to experience what took place at the original concerts, Mayer has also discussed himself as a case study of one who became a Deadhead in the After Jerry time period: "I approached the Dead from a completely different angle than most people who are older than me because I kind of represent this new generation of future Dead fans [who came into it] by way of the music only."[10]

As stated at the opening to this chapter, it is not because Mayer's experience is unique that there is value in examining his description of being a Deadhead. His experience is like that of so many others, but as a musician he is particularly insightful, and persuasive, in describing the power of the music. He puts it this way: "I consider myself no different than any other fan. I don't think I've had a more profound experience than anybody else discovering this music except that I have this reach on the guitar."[11]

7. Halperin, "Mayer Talks Grateful Dead," para. 3

8. Bones, "Mayer Talks New Album," 45:20.

9. Budnick, "Dead and Company Origin," para. 18.

10. Halperin, "Mayer Talks Grateful Dead," para. 3.

11. Halperin, "Mayer Talks Grateful Dead," para. 14.

Of course, that reach on the guitar meant that his subsequent experience was quite unlike that of every other fan.

FROM CONVERSION TO ACTION

Through a mutual contact, music producer Don Was, Mayer was afforded the chance to meet with Bob Weir and Mickey Hart. Mayer says he "sat down and sort of professed my love. I told them how this music had hit me. I wanted to tell them how much it meant to me."[12] These would be remarkable statements for anyone who only had a few years of exposure to the music. For such a testimony to come from an individual with such impressive credentials in composing and performing music is a powerful indicator that this is something more than a run-of-the-mill fan fascination with a favorite band.

John Mayer's stated feelings about this music must influence how we perceive his performances with Dead and Company. He is not just singing cover songs of another artist; he has effusively stated how much more they mean to him than other music. The added meaning that we know he attaches to this music will be elaborated on in chapter 12 as part of the discussion of the added levels of meaning that animate the movement.

Mayer has discussed in several interviews the influence that his Dead and Company bandmates have had in reorienting him to a more Deadhead approach to life. To avoid the risk that this work be taken over by John Mayer quotes, it is perhaps better to point to actual evidence of a change and not just repeat words. In this light, it is entirely remarkable that a songwriter and performer with his level of success would perform 259 concerts over ten years with that band and during those shows never once play one of his own songs. In his behavior he appears to emulate previous descriptions of the mentality of a convert; it is written, "Put on compassion, kindness, humility, gentleness, and patience" (Col 3:12).

12. Halperin, "Mayer Talks Grateful Dead," para. 6.

HOW FAR DOES THE ANALOGY STRETCH?

If it is instructive to relate John Mayer to the apostle Paul, what other parallels are there? There were, after all, twelve musicians who participated in the Grateful Dead over thirty years (half of them as keyboardist). Today Bob Weir and Phil Lesh might be thought of comparable to the apostles Peter and James: close associates of the founder who guide different sections of the faithful through the early decades of the movement's next phases. Pigpen might be cast as a John the Baptist character: a bit of a rough-edged precursor who exited the scene early.

Extended analogies are useful when they reveal new understanding. Every analogy can be stretched beyond the breaking point, and the exercise then must be abandoned when some features are found not to align. That a given analogy breaks down at some point, as all eventually will, does not diminish the insights gained from applying it where it does apply. To apply that guidance to the present case: that the analogy drawn between the Deadhead movement and the early days of the Jesus movement breaks down when pushed to extremes does not mean that the insights gained are less valuable.

The role of Robert Hunter is where the analogy falls apart and must be abandoned, though with the insights it provided still intact. Hunter's role, as lyricist for all of the great Garcia songs, cannot be overestimated. In many ways, it is the profound words of the songs that make this much more than musical entertainment for Deadheads. More on this topic in chapters 7 and 11 (a coincidence that Hunter would have appreciated).

The prominence of Hunter's role, and how it cracks the analogy mirror, clears the way to address the role of Garcia in the analogy. There is substantial risk of misunderstanding, when noting a parallel time course of the Deadhead and Christian movements, to refer to "the time after the founder." If we say that John Mayer is like Paul, does that imply that Garcia can be analogized to the founder of the Christian movement? Only to the extent that we can say that a highly charismatic personality made a lasting impact on a great many people.

No one who knew Garcia personally would have called him divine, though all would agree that the term "divinely inspired" would apply. That his artistic contribution could be judged more-than-mortal would not be exceptional in historical terms. It was not uncommon that the gifts of the greatest of Renaissance painters or classical composers be described as reflecting the divine. At the same time, saying so would not have implied that trait was attributed to the artist. As for the fealty of Deadheads for Garcia, it could be appropriately compared to the fervor shown by Shakespeare fans, the intensity of which has been termed "Bardolatry." In these other artistic realms, the fans need not fear they are committing some blasphemy if they describe some artist's work as being as close to the divine as a human may get.

There may be readers who would even take offense at Garcia's legacy being discussed in relation to that of Shakespeare or Michelangelo; time will tell if this is justified. What created the Deadhead phenomenon, though, was never just about Garcia, even musically. There is first the indispensable role that Hunter's lyrics play in instilling such deep feelings in the Deadheads. If we were to invert the historical analogy for a moment, it would be as if the Galilee movement was begun by one person who did the preaching alongside another who performed the signs and wonders. That's how significant Robert Hunter's role has been. On the music side, the magic was always in the interplay between all of the band members. No matter how highly one praises Garcia, it cannot be argued that there was anything about the Grateful Dead that was not a collaborative effort. Referring to Garcia as the founder of an ongoing movement holds no danger of crossing into blasphemy since he was never the unique creator of what was left behind.

The trait: Every Deadhead can describe, in detail, a particular occasion of listening to the music that was life-changing.

The comment: This topic would be a suitable one on which to begin a discussion with a Deadhead about what this all means. They likely will have been to many concerts that mean a great deal to them, but it is very common that one show in particular stands out. The level of detail they can recall, including who was with them, where they were in the concert venue, and which songs had an impact, reveals how deeply they were affected. The vividness of the memory, and the sensation experienced, will sound very much like many accounts given of born-again experiences. The lasting impact is very similar also, for it is written, "The fruit of the Spirit is love, joy, peace, patience, kindness, goodness, faithfulness, gentleness, and self-control. There is no law against such things" (Gal 5:22–23).

7

Shared Attributes of Deadheads

The passage: "Some believed the things which were spoken . . ." (Acts 28:24).

The context: The closing scenes in the book of Acts take place in Rome, which has been the destination of the entire second half of the narrative. The apostle Paul is under a comfortable form of house arrest, receiving local religious leaders and, as always, preaching the good news to them. As the quote above makes clear, that which has been true throughout the millennia was equally true then: what he had to say was not for everyone. But clearly some, and eventually many, did adopt his message and based their lives on it though they themselves were quite removed, in time and distance, from what took place in Galilee.

✝

The people who attend any large entertainment or sporting event can generally be expected to have more in common with one another than they do with anyone else they might come across who is not going to the same event. Depending on the size of the crowd and the type of event, we can expect commonalities in what people wear, the vehicles they drive, their type of residence, and likely even their hairstyles. No one would be surprised to find that those who attended a country music concert had more in common with one another than they have with those who attended a heavy metal show.

COMMON ATTRIBUTES OF A CROWD

The number of common attributes in the largest sports crowds might be more limited than would be found in the crowd at a concert. As the biggest sports crowds cut across all manner of demographics (for who does not like live sporting events?), the people in that crowd might only share a rough geography and some minimum level of disposable income—that, plus which color they wear to the stadium.

If one were to take a sample, on the day after a game, of a large football crowd and try to figure out what each person in the sample had in common, there would not be many clues to be found by observing their daily lives. Now suppose that a sample of the individuals in that crowd were brought together and informed that they had all been in the same stadium the previous day. It is not likely that any sort of meaningful interaction would take place between them after being given that news, beyond some pleasantries about the outcome of the contest.

The central premise of this work is that the common attributes of Deadheads are significant enough that a different result would be produced by this same crowd sample test. A crowd sample conducted on the day after a Dead event would not likely demonstrate a great deal more commonality in appearance than would be found among the football crowd (though back in the day, the original Grateful Dead crowds would have some conspicuous traits). Today such a Dead crowd sample might include the Fed chairman and a vegan vendor who just earned enough in the parking lot that day to buy a ticket to the show. If those two individuals were to encounter each other *without* knowing that they had been to the same event, the chances would not be good that they would strike up a friendly rapport (unless one of them were wearing a sign of their allegiance to the Dead, elaborated on in ch. 9). If, as in the previous crowd test, they were then told what it was that they had in common, the chances are excellent that, unlike the sports crowd, the Deadheads would know immediately that they had many similar attitudes and they would quickly fall to discussing them. This proposition cannot be proven other than by asking Deadheads if they think it is so.

If the two crowd samples in these thought experiments were mingled, and one wished to pick out those that had been at the football game and which at the concert, appearances alone would only help to discriminate a very few: not many of the itinerant hand-to-mouth vendors are likely to have set up shop near the NFL site. There is, however, a sure-fire way to pick out the normal-looking, non-itinerant Deadheads in the crowd: if a particularly catchy Grateful Dead song, such as "Ramble on Rose," were played in everyone's hearing, all of the Deadheads would begin to move in time with the music. They just can't help it. Some would do so subtly, some would not be so subtle.

COMMON ATTRIBUTES OF A DEADHEAD CROWD

It is a universal trait of Deadheads to want to dance along to the music. Such a statement would not seem necessary for the fans of a band that is known to produce dance music; surely it is not uncommon that all of the fans of certain musical acts like to dance when their music is playing. It is further likely, though, that the fans of dance band music would also dance when a variety of other bands and styles of music are playing; they just enjoy dancing. This is not always the case with Deadheads. Furthermore, while there are some Deadheads who will only dance to Grateful Dead music, there are also some songs that only Deadheads would dance to.

People who like to dance to a variety of musical types might not encounter many Grateful Dead songs that move them to dance, neither would they regard what some Deadheads are doing as dancing. But even when not overtly dancing in a way that others would recognize, there is a common rhythmic jangle in the way that Deadheads move whenever the music is playing. Sometimes it is no more explicit than the subtle groove that Jerry Garcia exhibited onstage, even during the most rousing of dance numbers. To see others swaying in that certain way is a very common and welcoming sight for Deadheads. As they approach a gathering of their fellows, and music is pouring out of one vehicle or another, everyone's movements begin to synchronize with the special rhythm to which they are all attuned.

What has been said about Deadheads in this chapter is not backed up by the kind of supporting data that has been presented in previous chapters. The validity of these statements made about dancing can be investigated by any interested party simply by visiting a Dead-themed event. That everyone moves in time to the music is immediately observable, as is the distinctive jangle the music brings out in their way of walking when not "dancing." What will remain a matter of conjecture for the observer is whether each Deadhead's manner of dancing would also be observed if a different style of music were playing.

ATTITUDES AND OBSERVABLE BEHAVIORS

This book puts forward the idea that there are more significant things that Deadheads have in common than that which is externally observable (e.g., frequency of consuming music from just one group, and dancing when they hear that music). The case study of John Mayer was presented as one example of what is being proposed here as a common attribute of Deadheads—that their feeling about this music is on a "deeper level" than for other music, and it represents an "extra dimension." Going from that documented example to saying that it must therefore also be true of others is to suggest that being a Deadhead is an all-or-none proposition, and that being a Deadhead, in large measure, means about the same thing to each of them. In a way it is to suggest that there is a predisposition to this behavior in a portion of the population and that Deadheads are born, not made. To put it more directly, was there something about John Mayer that made him ready to be a Deadhead before he heard "Althea" for the first time?

There are similar examples of an uneven distribution of extreme fandom in other realms. Suppose that three children in a household were taken to the same number of Little League baseball games, sat through the same number of music lessons, and received the same level of religious instruction and exposure. In later life, they all enjoy baseball, but only one checks the box scores each morning to see how each player did; they all enjoy listening to music, but only one will go to great lengths to play music with friends at every opportunity; and each keeps up with religious observances, but only one of those lives has been committed to religious service. So it might be if they each had the same exposure to the Grateful Dead: only one sibling now orders every new CD release, checks the setlist for which songs have been played on tour, and looks for opportunities to see the cover bands in town. It would be readily accepted that the baseball fan would have some common attitudes with other baseball fans, the musician with other musicians, and the one with the religious calling would have similar attitudes and some affinity to others who have made a similar dedication of their lives. In the same way it should make sense that those with the stealie-shaped keyhole in their brain (see ch. 9) have more in common with other Deadheads than just a way of walking in time to the music.

SO MANY SHOWS, SO MUCH DATA

A notable feature of the Deadhead way of being is a high level of interest in tracking and analyzing the lists of songs that the band played. This is not a universal trait but is a common enough that it was also discussed in chapter 3 in relation to commonalities with baseball fans. Just as there is a wide variation among baseball fans in their interest in employing new-style advanced statistics, so there are those Deadheads who wish to minutely document all that took place (musically) at each Dead-themed show, and there are, in contrast, those who are "feelers, not knowers."

While not universal to all Deadheads, interest in setlist minutiae is something of a hallmark trait of the group. It could be that this would also be a trait of fans of other musical acts, but in those cases there isn't anything to track or analyze; every night's performance has the same list of songs played in exactly the same order.

For those Deadheads who are serious about data tracking, the internet age has facilitated deeper and more esoteric levels of exploration. The interest and effort expended toward precise concert documentation, though, certainly did not begin with the digital age but goes way back to the days of the printed page. Grateful Dead fans produced several long-running newsletters (most notably *The Golden Road* and *Dupree's Diamond News*) that included the sorts of features and up-to-date band news that one would expect of fan clubs. Among the regular items in each issue, they also published concert setlists covering several months of shows at a time. Why would someone be interested in reading about which songs were played, in which sequence, at a concert several months back, which that person had not attended? Fans who undertook such scrutiny were rewarded by discovering that the band often had intentions and a hidden plan in the song selection—for example, concerts in St. Louis, more often than not, included a song written by native son Chuck Berry.

There is abundant evidence that there has always been a keen interest, among some, in knowing what was played at past shows. In addition to the newsletters as a source of information, a complete listing of all shows and all songs, the Deadbase, was first published in 1987 by John W. Scott, Mike Dolgushkin, and Stu Nixon. This work went through nineteen printings over twenty-eight years before moving online. Today elaborate web-based databases (e.g., Setlists.net) can query how often combinations of songs were played in different years or even by day of week (it is true that certain songs are more likely to be played on Sunday). A similar level of detailed data is also gathered for the growing number of jam bands that follow the program of varying their playlist for each performance.

SONG LYRICS AND THE "DEEPER LEVEL"

An important shared characteristic of Deadheads, one of those that cannot be evaluated with data, is that they have a deep appreciation for the lyrics of the Grateful Dead songs. While the intention of this work is not to probe the lyrics for their hidden philosophy or religiosity, it is the case that the world described in those lyrics is one that is comfortable to Deadheads. Just as was the case with the band's singular approach to performance of and recording music, the lyrics of Dead songs have some distinct features compared to those of other bands of their era. The most common themes in typical rock and roll songs—of the ups and downs of romantic love, of thrill-seeking and fast living in fast cars, teen angst and daring—these themes never appear in the Grateful Dead view of the world. With their origins in folk music, the more common themes in Grateful Dead music are the struggles of simple people rather than the challenges of being a modern teen. Robert Hunter and John Barlow, the principal lyric writers who collaborated with the musicians, were well past their own teen struggles when they began contributing their work to the band. Their creations, though sometimes cryptic, more often relate to the interior adventures of those who came of age in the 1960s, or in a '60s-influenced culture.

How listeners, especially Deadheads, react to the topic of the lyrics is surely a mingling of elements of the nature/nurture dichotomy referred to above: do listeners respond immediately to the messages of these songs because of who they themselves are, or have they been influenced by repeated exposure to a type of song? A leaning toward the Deadhead view of life can become reinforced when the listener perceives that there is a population of other Deadheads out there who see the world similarly.

Robert Hunter very often wrote highly poetic lyrics that invited many possible interpretations, so much so that it has long been something of a talmudic hobby of Deadheads to compare what they hear in various phrases and figures of speech. After a few experiences of realizing that the lyrics mean much more than they appear to on the surface, the listeners hone their own interpretive skills. It might actually be the case that a person comes to recognize themselves as a Deadhead only when particularly cryptic lyrics begin to make sense.

When perceived through a Deadhead's understanding of the world, certain lines from the song "Bertha" mean something to a Deadhead that they might not to another listener.[1] At about the midpoint of that song, the main character arrays himself in a certain color, goes to visit the shore, and sets about trying to interpret things that do not make sense on the surface. Though no two Deadheads might agree on that meaning, they know the song is about something of importance. A further idea, that quite a number of Hunter's song lyrics are specifically about the Deadhead experience, is explored further in chapter 11.

SOME SHARED ATTRIBUTES

Once the notion is accepted that Deadheads share some characteristics and attitudes, the challenge becomes one of identifying those traits that are not easily observable. In the many news reports, articles, and books on the subject, generalizations hold sway over data. Lacking reliable evidence, a special approach will be taken here, specifically for the Jesus followers that are the intended audience of this work. That special approach is the same taken in other chapters by making reference to the Scripture of the after-Jesus time period but not without first making a detour into the meaning of a Greek word from that time.

One of the most commonly used words in the writings about Jesus is the Greek word *agape*, usually translated simply as "love" (and pronounced uh-*gah*-pay). This is the word used by the

---

1. The current practice of administering the copyrights to song lyrics strongly discourages making many quotations in print, and so reference will be made to illustrative lyrics; readers will be encouraged to look them up for themselves.

apostle Paul in the passage that has been so often used in wedding ceremonies: agape is kind, patient, etc. But agape is not the only word in Greek for love, and it's meaning did not include the romantic love celebrated at weddings; that would be "eros." Rather, agape represents the type of love that Jesus meant when he gave his toughest instruction, to "love your enemies." Agape is also the operative word in the familiar verse "God so loved the world . . ." This is not generally the sense that young lovers have in mind as they plan their wedding.

There is no comprehensive or convincing way to summarize the common characteristics of Deadheads, from so many walks of life, who enjoy a special fellowship when they gather. A suitable approximation can be made however, by borrowing the list of attributes that Paul used to characterize agape, divine love. By maintaining usage of the original Greek word in 1 Cor 13:4–8 below, it is suggested that the reader reconsider these attributes not as marriage vows but as behavioral traits that are common to a group of people.

> *Agape* is patient and kind;
> *agape* does not envy nor boast, and is not proud;
> *agape* does not dishonor others and is not self-seeking;
> *agape* is not easily angered and keeps no record of wrongs;
> *agape* does not delight in evil but revels in the truth;
> *agape* protects, trusts in all, hopes in all, always perseveres;
> *agape* never ends.

The bond among Deadheads is such that each of them will recognize themselves, and the universal Deadhead spirit, in that list. This list is not meant to be exhaustive nor exclusive. There certainly are other traits one might ascribe as being common to Deadheads, a sense of humor being high on the list. And it goes without saying, as is true for the broad generalizations made in each chapter, that no claim is made that this is unique to Deadheads. For the purposes of this book, though, to give Christians a sense of the common characteristics they will find in every Deadhead they meet, this list is hard to top.

Simple statements are usually best, whether they be ancient or modern. A summary of these characteristics, using the original ancient language to avoid overfamiliarity, might be found in the most direct, yet challenging, instruction: agape one another.

A simple challenge from a modern source comes from one of the Grateful Dead's signature, self-referential songs, "Uncle John's Band." There are profound questions posed at the end of each of the four verses of the song, and the first simply asks whether the listener is kind. A more recent instance of the band giving a simple but profound ethical imperative came at the conclusion of the last of the Fare Thee Well performances in Chicago's Soldier Field in 2015. Mickey Hart stepped up to the microphone to issue a parting message to all the gathered faithful, something that was very rarely done by a band notoriously sparse with on stage banter or introductions. At that concluding event, though, Mickey imparted this final thought to the crowd: "Be kind."[2]

The trait: Deadheads all love to dance.

The comment: It is possible to go out and verify that this is a common trait without interacting with any particular individuals. By going to where Dead music is playing, one can observe, at a population level, the Deadheads all moving at the same frequency. There is, to be sure, variation in the amount of movement each individual is making, and a good deal of the "dancing" taking place is done without moving the feet. That communal joy cannot be better described than it was many years ago when it was written, "Don't be slack in enthusiasm; let the Spirit boil over" (Rom 12:11); and again, "Rejoice always. Pray continually. Be grateful in every situation" (1 Thess 5:16–18).

---

2. The Capitol Theatre. "12 Unforgettable Moments," no. 12.

8

Sinners and Outcasts

The passage: "At that time a huge persecution began . . ." (Acts 8:1).

The context: The relationship of Christians to civil authorities is a long and complicated one. The founder of the movement, of course, is reported in each Gospel as continually sparring with those who perceived his peace and love movement to be a threat; it did not end well. His immediate followers were, ineffectively, detained and beaten to stop them from spreading their message, as referenced in the passages introducing chapters 1 and 4. The passage attached to this chapter comes later in Acts and reports a more generalized response that took place on the same day as the killing of the first martyr, Saint Stephen. As the movement spread throughout the Roman Empire from its modest origins, a new set of issues with authorities developed, the history of which is checkered. With the passage of time, the movement grew to become the dominant group in many societies and they, in turn, then proceeded to use temporal power to persecute other groups.

✝

The purpose of this work is to encourage Christians to engage in dialogue with Deadheads in order that they might learn how much they have in common. A further suggestion, so that a true sense of the community in action can be had, is that observers go to visit Deadheads in their native element: the parking lots where they gather before concerts. Some would-be visitors will likely have concerns that doing so will bring them in proximity to activities that they do not approve of and are not comfortable being around. The reputation of many rock and roll bands and their fans is that they live outside the moral code that most churchgoers would advocate. In the case of the Dead, they were notoriously associated, from their earliest days, with the "anything goes" ethos of the hippie culture of San Francisco, especially the Haight-Ashbury scene. As is so often the case, a little biblical perspective can help.

Jesus was notorious for mixing and mingling with people that were deemed objectionable by the religious hierarchy of his day. The Gospels' stories are chock full of outrage being expressed by proper, upstanding people over the company that Jesus kept. In most of these accounts, two objectionable groups are mentioned: those who are termed sinners and those who are regarded as socially unacceptable. For a Christian today who is evaluating their own comfort level in mixing with people who are not likely ever to be found in church, a meaningful distinction might be made about behaviors that transgress a moral code (sinners) versus behaviors that violate a legal or societal standard (outcasts). Yet further distinctions might be needed concerning activities that were once illegal but no longer are, depending on your jurisdiction.

PROHIBITION 2.0

Prohibition has a spotty history in the United States. For thirteen years it was illegal to produce, import, or sell alcoholic beverages in the United States. Legal restrictions on commercial activity, while they lasted, were not directed at the individual citizen's actions when it came to consumption. One has to believe that many devout churchgoers were among those who did not let the new laws change their behavior, though the apostle Paul does list "drunkards" among those who will not be part of God's kingdom (1 Cor 6:10). In our own day, there are church establishments that focus solely on the parts of that passage that refer to objectionable sexual practices without mentioning the references to drinking. ("Greedy" people are also on that list of the objectionable; it would make for an interesting study to determine whether there are any churches that have taken to banishing the greedy from their ranks.)

A contrast might be drawn between how the churchgoing public reacted to the two social policy initiatives: prohibition of the sale of alcohol on the one hand, and the campaign, which quickly succeeded the end of alcohol prohibition, that made cannabis illegal throughout the country. Legal restrictions on cannabis are now being eased, state by state, but there is lingering societal disapproval of it, a holdover of decades of government misinformation. Cannabis consumption had never been as entrenched in society as alcohol was, which likely contributed to law-abiding church folk believing that the government's legal prohibition of cannabis made sense.

It was not always so. Eli Lilly and Company was among the prominent legal sellers of cannabis through the 1920s. Lilly's own cultivated variety, *Cannabis americana*, was in part developed by the grandson of the founder of the firm. Also named Eli Lilly (and also a company president), that second Eli Lilly had done his thesis work in cannabis pharmacology and saw a future in it.[1] It was not until 1937 that the federal government took action against its distribution.

This belated action by the government was not taken in response the appearance of a shocking new phenomenon in society. Cannabis use is well-documented throughout human recorded history, including by Herodotus, the "father of history." It was Herodotus who first introduced the term cannabis into European languages in describing its use in mystical rituals.[2] When the Nixon administration took action to classify it as among the most dangerous substances available (schedule 1), it had nothing

1. Wren, "Eli Lilly."
2. Butrica, "Cannabis Among the Greeks," 54–55.

whatever to do with a newer, better scientific understanding of the substance or its effects.[3] No, it had everything to do with cynical effort to develop new means of harassing the elements of society the administration wished to target. It's worth asking whether the decades-long cannabis misinformation campaign contributed to a loss of government credibility on these topics, ultimately undermining their warnings about opioid compounds, with vast consequences still unfolding.

There is a flip side of the legal-versus-moral assessment when it comes to drug distribution: the entirely unexaggerated horrors of the opioid epidemic. This flood of newly synthesized substances is the result of drug company development programs, which were legal—sanctioned by the federal government—but about which moral questions are now being raised. Scrutiny is increasingly being applied to the actions of those that profited from widespread distribution of compounds, so carefully designed and manufactured, without regard for potential harm. The wreckage of so many lives that has come from abuse of legal pharmaceuticals dwarfs the harms done by cannabis overuse.

TARGETED ENFORCEMENT

The exaggerated horrors used by prohibitionists to try to scare the public off cannabis proved counterproductive to their credibility on what was good for society's youth. In an attempt to make examples out of those who were seen as undermining social order, the Grateful Dead, and other bands and artists, were made targets by police, resulting in a number of run ins on possession charges. These uneven enforcement efforts were not in response to any out-of-control or dangerous level of abuse by famous musicians. They were, rather, goal directed toward publicity. In the end, the authorities efforts likely had the opposite effect to what they intended: bands and individuals that suffered set-up busts became heroes of the countercultural movement.

3. See Neal, "Up in Smoke?"

High profile individuals at least had the advantage of competent legal support in dealing with drug charges; this was not the case for most of their fans. For many years, local authorities also had enforcement programs targeting individuals who attended Grateful Dead concerts, with serious prison sentences often resulting. Whether any such actions in the War on Drugs ever proved more beneficial than harmful, to any individual or society, is doubtful.

SINNERS? OR OUTCASTS?

The gradual move of cannabis into the cultural mainstream in recent decades has paralleled the shift in perceptions of the Grateful Dead (and Deadheads). Those who were once counterculture pariahs are frequently now described as cultural icons. Should the willingness of Christians to visit Deadhead gatherings be affected by the changing legal status of the activities commonly enjoyed there? As the legal status shifts along with attitudes, there is a need to draw a distinction between the actions of outcasts on one hand, as violators of laws and social norms, and sinners, as violators of moral codes in terms of harm to individuals and society.

An alternative standard, behavioral rather than statutory, may be the right approach to determining whether to keep company with those whose ways are different. It is, of course, not realistic to try to entirely avoid the company of sinners; that is surely the path to a lonely existence. A sound Christian approach to evaluating others' actions would be look out for behaviors that do harm to self or others. This approach was recommended by Jesus in Matt 7:17–20, when he advised judging the quality of the fruit as the way to evaluate the tree.

In surveying crowd behavior, the amount of damage done to persons and property at an alcohol-fueled event (e.g., NASCAR events or football games) will likely compare unfavorably with that done at a Dead scene. The stark difference is not only evident at large stadium gatherings; while "bar fight" is a common expression, a "weed fight" is not something one hears about very often. And though the quantity of laughing gas balloons consumed by some Deadheads can be unappealing, it is unlikely that this has seriously harmed anyone nor contributed to as many car accidents as alcohol consumption surely does.

POSITIVE EXAMPLES ON THE LOT

There are abundant positives to be witnessed, for those with eyes to see, in the parking lot of a Dead-related event. The itinerant caravan is thriving. Vendors are there with arts and crafts products of every possible description. Food cooked on site is plentiful, performers of various stripes delight passersby, and fellowship is evident in every smile. An objective evaluation of the life of itinerants must conclude that their industriousness and their ability to survive by their wits, over many years and many miles, has not been diminished by their choice of recreational products. For this community to have coexisted on the road, show after show, year after year, is evidence that a strong ethical code prevails among them. The most general conclusion to be drawn from an open-minded, behavioral assessment of the "Outcasts" seen in the parking lots can be found in another passage where it is written, "Those who practice righteousness are righteous" (1 John 3:7).

INDIVIDUAL HARMS

The thriving vendor scene in the parking lots of Dead-related events provides abundant counterevidence to the predictions made by antidrug crusaders of the wreckage of lives that will come to those who did not heed their warnings. This is not to say that there are not a significant number of individuals who *are* harmed by overuse (though this is as true for alcohol as for Deadheads' preferred intoxicants). There is also not much reason to believe that the bad consequences of overuse are more of a problem for Dead fans than for the fans of other bands, or that these individuals would not be in the same condition if the Grateful Dead had never existed.

The performers, as much as the fans, are susceptible to overuse, and the tragic stories of the demise of many rock and roll stars are well known. Overindulgence seems to be a shared risk for those that make a living by sharing their emotions. The list of performers who have suffered through overconsumption is certainly not limited to rock bands that originated in the '60s drug culture, nor limited to just the musical world. It is in that context that we should consider the addictions that Jerry Garcia struggled with, to a greater degree than his bandmates. Garcia had tried several rounds of rehab to address his drug consumption and had better and worse years toward the end of his life. Though he outlived many of the more notorious rock performers to come out of the 1960s, his overconsuming lifestyle almost certainly contributed to his heart giving out at age fifty-three.

$$\textit{\textcircled{7}}$$

The trait: There are no mean Deadheads.

The comment: This statement presents the challenge of proving a negative proposition (since the absence of evidence is not the same as evidence of absence), as was the case for the trait in chapter 4. Searching for a counterexample is not likely to be a rewarding enterprise. A different approach could be to ask Deadheads if they ever remember making the acquaintance of a fellow Head that they found to be a mean-spirited person. More than likely that person will respond that all those they have ever known would be better described as a person who would try to "comfort the discouraged, help the weak, be patient with all" (1 Thess 5:14), and again would be one to heed what was written: "In humility regard others as better than yourselves. Let each of you look not to your own interests, but to the interests of others" (Phil 2:3–4).

9

Signification

The passage: "Greet all with a holy kiss . . ." (1 Thess 5:26).

The context: It's been said that there is nothing more annoying than a new Christian. But what was it like when *all* of the Christians were new ones? As Paul writes to the communities springing up all around the Mediterranean, he expresses genuine heartfelt affection for them and encourages them to do the same. Over time, the early community was replaced by the church, which, sadly, has come to be perceived as more interested in enforcing rules for everyday living than on spreading peace and love.

✝

Way back in the fall of 1984, Don Henley had a hit song titled "The Boys of Summer." That song included a lyric about seeing a Cadillac that had the unusual marking of a Deadhead sticker. The theme of that song is one of nostalgia and regret over lost love; the connection seems to be that there is something to be lamented about a Grateful Dead symbol on a high-end vehicle. By assuming that the listeners will understand the meaning of the symbol, the inclusion of this reference in the song makes several points about the Deadhead phenomenon.

DEADHEAD STICKERS

In the 1984 song, seeing a Deadhead sticker on a vehicle is taken to be a commonplace observation; it is really the specific type of vehicle that the singer sees as worthy of comment. Seeing a Deadhead sticker on public display actually is routine because Deadheads have such a propensity for letting people know who they are no matter where they are. The sticker that was observed on the Cadillac was not for Henley's band, the Eagles, nor was it a CSNY sticker, nor The Doors, etc. (Such sightings would be about as odd as a book that contains only a single exclamation point!) As was the case with other data presented, the point is *not* that Grateful Dead stickers are the only band bumper stickers one will see; the Rolling Stone tongue is one that can still be seen. It is that the frequency of seeing Dead references today (if one can recognize all of them) is far, far higher than would be expected based only on the record sales that the band achieved decades ago. Why are they the band with bumper stickers on display, continually, and now more than forty years after being mentioned in a song?

Deadheads like to show their colors, whether it be on a Cadillac or on a scooter. By the tone of Henley's song, it seems that we are to assume he saw a relatively new Cadillac, in good repair, rather than a vehicle that showed signs of having crisscrossed the country on multiple concert tours. We are also to assume that the owner of the Cadillac placed the sticker there, and it was not actually the subversive act of a child of the car owner. All of these alternate scenarios are likely to have occurred somewhere or other. The evidence is that, among the things that Deadheads do most reliably, right after always wanting to hear more Dead music and dance to it, is let the world know of their presence.

The specific wording of the song lyric has some significance for this topic. The item is identified as a "Deadhead sticker," not a Grateful Dead sticker. Maybe that wording just fit the meter of the song, but it serves to put the attention on the person sending the signal as opposed to a band or record company promotional effort (relating to points made in ch. 1). The implications are that anyone can recognize what a Deadhead sticker is even without the name of the band being mentioned and, further, that the person listening to the song is (a) familiar with what Deadheads are and (b) has expectations of what vehicle they might be likely to drive. The Cadillac is a disconnect.

Ultimately what the song lyric demonstrates is that Deadheads have more in common with one another on the inside (wanting to share their attitude with the world) than on the outside (what car they drive); evidently this was true in 1984 and it is becoming more so with each passing decade. What would Don Henley's reaction be to the chairman of the Federal Reserve discussing Dead concerts in congressional testimony? Is that in any way a bad thing? Would the world be a better place if Deadheads remained marginalized, or even had ceased to exist?

VARIETIES OF SIGNS

The most common type of Deadhead sign that might have been on that Cadillac forty years ago is an exaggerated drawing of a skull that has a lightning bolt dividing the interior of the skull, splitting it into red and blue fields. As will be described further below, this image has come to be termed a "stealie," especially when Deadheads personalize the internal field to reflect their own interests. Alternatively, the sticker that indicated a Deadhead was on board the car in the song might have been one that incorporates cartoon versions of marching (or dancing) teddy-bear style creatures, often in varied colors; or it could have been turtle-looking creatures (terrapins to be exact) standing on two legs on dry ground and playing instruments (and dancing, always dancing). The Deadhead symbol might also have been images of skeletons, playing musical instruments, perhaps tipping an Uncle Sam top hat at a rakish angle, or perhaps just dancing in a line together.

Though these many forms of signaling do not include the name of the band, each would be recognized by all other Deadheads for what they are. There are still further means of signaling between Deadheads intended to be understood *only* by people who are steeped in all of the iconography. One prominent example is the handprint of Jerry Garcia, distinctive and recognizable due to the loss of half of his finger in a childhood accident. The image of Garcia's hand was used as cover art on one of his solo albums and has since migrated to graphics displayed in concert, innumerable bumper stickers, T-shirts and every other manner of craft for sale in the parking lot bazaar.

A newer form of cryptic signaling on T-shirts is to modify well-known brands and corporate logos so that they convey lyrics and song titles that Deadheads would recognize. One example is the colorful and familiar Mountain Dew logo that has been repurposed by modifying it to "Morning Dew," the title of one the band's landmark numbers. In similar manner, the Stella Artois artwork has been modified to "Stella Blue," another foundation stone of the repertoire. A person unfamiliar with these song titles would likely not even look closely enough at the artwork to notice that the familiar logo had been modified. Only an observer who is familiar with the titles of a good many Grateful Dead songs would get the true message. The same is true of many obscure song lyrics that appear on bumper stickers, or even more obscure messages along the lines of "My other vehicle is a Dark Star / Lovelight."

SIGNS AT THE SHOW

The exhibition of all these varied manner of symbols and signals is found throughout the concert venues themselves. One could reliably follow the gradient of increasing occurrence of Dead-themed attire to find your way to the event where the Deadheads were gathering. Not that this is unusual: it is a more and more common sight at all pop and rock concerts, as well as at sporting events, for fans to wear apparel that shows the fan's devotion to their favorites. Deadheads are no exception in wearing their allegiance on their sleeves, as it were, when attending musical events, but this is very much a phenomenon of the last few decades at concerts and at sporting events.

Whereas today the fan who does not wear team merchandise is the exception at a professional or college sporting event (hard to tell the difference these days), it was not always so. Photos and television recordings of the crowds at sporting events even into the 1980s showed that very few fans wore team merchandise. Likewise, while it is a common site for attendees at twenty-first century Dead events to don some impressive tie-dyed attire, evidence in photos and film footage of daylight Grateful Dead events shows most of the crowd in simple T-shirts or flannel shirts, much like the band. Tie-dyed shirts were the exception, worn by those who were living the alternate lifestyle full time. Today the tie-dyed attire is a convenient way for the concertgoers who spend their days in the straight world to go out at night and let their freak flag fly.

WHY SIGNAL?

Two phenomena have been described here: overt signaling at public gatherings by, for example, pulling out the tie-dye shirt, and more individual signaling, even to the point of being cryptic, which is directed only to others in the know. The same impulse for the group cohesion experienced in a crowd all similarly dressed at sporting events certainly shapes Deadhead attire at concert events. Individuals bring their own identity to it by choosing shirts that recall particular prior concerts or favorite performers, much as sports fans will wear the jersey number of a favored player or the jersey design of a preferred era of the team.

Sports fans also signal their allegiance outside of stadium events by means of car decals, hats and shirts, screen savers—you name it. In rough terms, the frequency of the fans' private signaling is related to the historic success of the team: people signal about something they are proud to be associated with. This measure again points to the distinctness of the Deadhead propensity to signal. The likelihood of individuals being engaged in Deadhead signaling is entirely out of proportion to the commercial success that the band ever enjoyed. How many Steely Dan or Eagles bumper stickers does one see? Look around and you will notice that Deadheads behave differently.

An apt comparator for the Deadheads' propensity to signal may be the veterans of the United States Marine Corps. There are only half as many service members in the Marines as in the Navy, and yet it is much more common to see hats, shirts, bumper stickers and flags flying outside of homes that identify ex-Marines. Their inclination to want to want to be identified as ex-Marines must say something about what that experience meant, and continues to mean, to them. Compared to the average Navy or Army veteran, Marines are more likely to want to be identified as such, and they exhibit an eagerness to engage with strangers on that topic.

A comparison more related to the theme of this work would be the practice of many Christians to wear a visible cross around the neck to let others know how important their faith is to them. Not many Deadheads are seen wearing a symbol of their allegiance all day, every day, as some committed religious folks do, but there are older Christian practices that may be more relevant. The ancient use of the fish symbol was a way for Christians to identify one another and provided a discrete way to recognize one another in a way that was cryptic to those not in the know. Today Deadheads have no reason to fear being discovered, but the inclination to want to subtly identify one another motivates the use of sometimes sly messaging.

STEALIE SELF-EXPRESSION

The most recognizable Grateful Dead symbol is the sketch of the skull with lightning bolt through the center cavity. The sketch had originally been used as a decal to mark the band's equipment on the road. It was then used as the cover artwork for the 1974 album titled *Steal Your Face*. That album title comes from a line in one of the band's songs ("He's Gone") though that song does not appear on that live album. That original sketch, along with the thousands of variations personalized by Deadheads, is known as a "stealie," in reference to the album title.

In the most personalized of stealies, the lightning bolt in the center cavity is replaced by a symbol that relates to the individual: city or state flags, college mascots, any manner of hobbies, even religious symbols. The general frame of the sketch is also modifiable to any artist's taste or fancy. A casual image search for "stealie art" will yield truly bountiful results. A few features are left in common in all of them: the bare outline of the skull cavity and the eye sockets and teeth. Those elements are a shared formalism that connects all the stunning degree of varied expression.

The manifold artistic expression within the constraints of the stealie frame embodies the unlimited individuality that is contained within shared Deadhead identity. Each personal stealie is a way to declare oneself to be a Deadhead first and then to highlight other fascinating personal dimensions of one's life, which are entirely compatible and complementary. But if the other dimensions of one's life are the focus of the artistic expression, why frame them in a stealie at all? Because of that "extra dimension" of meaning that being a Deadhead entails, as described in the chapter 6 conversion story. And because every Deadhead who is signaling, by any of these forms discussed, feels compelled to let others know of that extra dimension. Many a Scripture illustration, which stress the imperative of evangelizing, could be inserted here. Instead, the last word will be given to the instructions sent to Deadheads (written "Dead Heads" in the original usage) in the band's first fan newsletter in 1967: "Every chance you get, proceed to herald the Grateful Dead records as marvelous super—to radio stations and record stores and anyone else you see on the street."[1]

$$\textcircled{\mathcal{T}}$$

The Deadhead trait: Deadheads own several items of band-themed merchandise that were not sold by the band.

---

1. GDSets.com, "GD Newsletter 1967," para. 9.

Signification

The comment: The Grateful Dead's business practices, such as they were, seem to have inadvertently contributed to their longevity as a cultural force. Not unlike those professional baseball teams that found that widespread TV access to their product contributed to, rather than diminished, the crowds attending games in person, so did the band's tolerance for fans' taping and distributing copies of their live concerts have the effect of multiplying their fan base. That same benign neglect has contributed to the vast proliferation of every conceivable modification of Grateful Dead imagery, resulting in a very potent grassroots marketing effort. In displaying their Dead-themed merchandise, Deadheads can encourage others, as was written long ago, to "be of the same mind, having the same love, being in full accord and of one mind" (Phil 2:2).

IO

Liturgy

The passage: "Passing down to you that which I received . . ." (1 Cor 11:23).

The context: Paul's writing about the practices at the communion meal are the earliest record of what has now been faithfully repeated billions of times around the world when Christians share the bread and cup. His formulation of the words of institution do not differ greatly from those in the Gospel accounts, suggesting that a common oral tradition is their source. Paul's language in this passage, however, is emphatic in stating that he received it from the Lord. How, exactly, this happened is not spelled out.

✝

The previous chapter detailed the many types of signals used by Deadheads to let the world know of their allegiance to a band that has been out of business for thirty years. Many of those car decals, T-shirts, etc. make clever use of wording and images to hint at, but not use, the name of the band. There is one message, though, now commonly used over many decades, that does name the band and says a great deal about why Deadheads are the way they are: "There is NOTHING like a Grateful Dead concert." This statement first appeared in print in the liner notes for the Europe '72 live album and is attributed to one of the early saints of the movement, Willy Legate.

FACTORS MAKING DEAD SHOWS UNIQUE

Earlier chapters have already detailed the ways in which the concerts the Grateful Dead performed were different from those of their contemporaries: a different list of songs each night, and even the same songs were performed uniquely each time. They never had the intent to make them sound "just like the album." The long improvisation jams were the highlight of the shows, something that was not done by other rock bands until the Grateful Dead had established the precedent (and demonstrated that there was an audience for it).

The statement of nothing else being like those shows meant much more than a unique approach to song choice in concerts. By itself, the "NOTHING like" statement wouldn't seem like a message that many fans would want to proudly attach to their car if it only meant that their favorite band is the only one to play a unique setlist every night. The deeper message is that those concerts meant more to their fans than what they experienced at other types of performances. There was that "extra dimension" involved that compelled the fans to travel many a mile to experience it again and again.

Some of what made the concerts so impactful was the structure to the overall concert. While the exact list of songs varied, the organization of the songs into sections of the concert became standardized, formalized even, and became an expected part of the experience. Just as the individualized stealies described in the previous chapter are unique expressions within a standardized frame or template, so each concert, unique in its setlist, was structured just like the other shows in its arrangement. The organization, or architecture of the concert, has been carried forward by Dead and

Company and by the many succeeding bands that reproduce the Grateful Dead concert experience. It has become as formalized as the idea that great symphonies should have four movements, and the four movements are expected to have predictable properties in terms of tempo and tone.

THE TWO-SET FORMALISM

From the mid-70's onward, the Grateful Dead adhered to a concert form that included two sets, with a longish break in between, plus one encore song. There were some exceptional circumstances in which an acoustic set was added, as had been the pattern in the earliest days. The form could also be modified to accommodate a guest performer of the stature of Bob Dylan. The two-set convention, however, became the standard for their nearly twenty final performing years, many of which are regarded as being their finest. That two-set form has now been strictly adhered to by Dead and Company for their two-hundred-plus shows.

The two sets of songs are conveniently referred to as the first set and the second set. The first set is made up of a collection of crowd favorites, varying in tempo, length, and amount of freestyle jamming in each. Frequently in the current scenario, several of the first-set songs will be ones that the crowd enthusiastically joins in on, singing the chorus and giving emphasis to favorite lines. Songs with an appropriate geographic reference for the venue will be found in the first set, and if there is an overall theme to the songs chosen for the night, it will be evident there.

The show reaches its high point at the end of the second set, followed by a single encore song then tacked on (occasionally more than one on special nights). In the concerts of many other rock acts, the band's most popular, signature songs are saved to be played last, as one of multiple encores; as crowd favorites, they represent a high point of the evening. In the case of Dead and related bands, encore songs are a wind down: they contain neither long jams nor thundering crescendos. Just a one-and-done to get the crowd on their way with all drama previously concluded. In the current style of Dead and Company, the encore songs have high emotional content, reflective of the shared musical experience, but they are not the focus of the performance.

THE STRUCTURE OF THE SECOND SET

The unique features of the second set are what most distinguish Dead shows from other pop and rock concerts. It is what occurs in the second set, typically, that produces the intense personal experiences that keep Deadheads coming back for more. The second set is distinguished from the first by the songs included and by the way the songs are played but also by the music played that would not meet the formal definition of a song. In the second set, all of the songs are vehicles for extended jams, and the band can be counted on to glide from one song to another through improvisational bridges without a break in the music.

More than the way the songs are played, and for how long, the second set is distinctive for its non-song offerings. In the middle of the second set there will always be a point at which the instrumentalists leave the stage and the drummers (always more than one) commence an extended percussion performance. In recent years that segment has included a newly invented electronic apparatus that produces a range of vibrations unique to the Dead universe. By convention, the percussion interlude is termed Drums in each show's published setlist and in the parlance among all Deadheads.

Drums is followed by a segment that is termed Space. This is the free exploration of the entirety of sounds that can be produced by guitars and electronic keyboards. Ever so slowly, the rudiments of harmony, melody, and syncopation will emerge, but no one is in a rush. The audience is asked to indulge the performers' uninhibited experimentation along the outer bounds of the sound/music horizon. Ample room is left for muses, individual and collective, to bring forth new expressions of their inspiration. This can appear like the musicians getting a little R & R amidst the strain of constant traveling and playing everyone else's favorite song; during Space they can reconnect with their deepest love of music, tap in to its origins, and join their bandmates in an open conduit to a new creation.

Space gradually, gracefully, takes on the dimensions of music rather than sound. This transition becomes distinct when the drummers rejoin the group (after their break) and begin to add some rhythm to the soundscape that the instrumentalists have conjured. From there, at a deliberate pace, there is a transition to one of a select group of songs that occupy the slot of "the song after Space."

WHAT COMES AFTER SPACE

Analysis of years of Grateful Dead setlists demonstrate that certain songs typically occur later in the show than others (though if there is one statement that can be made with certainty about the world of the Grateful Dead, it is that there are *no* hard and fast rules). In the standard sequence for the second set, songs with long (some *very* long) jams are followed by the Drums interlude, then Space, then one of the Sorrowful Songs (described below), and then a shift back to freewheeling, dance inducing, joy-reflecting rock and roll. Every Deadhead knows the sequence, but in the course of a particular show they are ready to be surprised by which particular song occupies each specific slot.

Setlist.fm has graciously provided data on the average position in the set for each song performed by the Grateful Dead, as well as the number of times each song was played. They provide the same information for all of the Dead and Company shows through 2023. As will be shown, the pattern for which songs occur toward the end of the second set has been scrupulously maintained in the recent concerts. In the tables below, asterisks mark those songs on the lists occurring after Space for both the Grateful Dead and for Dead and Company. For the Grateful Dead, Space was listed 1,061 times at an average set position of 15.06. For Dead and Company, Space was listed 228 times at an average set position of 14.1.

Liturgy

Table 3. Average Set Position of Sorrowful Songs for Grateful Dead and Dead and Company

Grateful Dead		
Avg. Set Position	Times Played	Song Title
15.1	74	Standing on the Moon*
15.4	113	China Doll
15.5	347	Black Peter*
15.9	260	The Wheel
16.0	562	The Other One
16.7	268	Throwing Stones
17.5	326	Stella Blue*
17.7	41	The Weight*
17.7	137	It's All Over Now Baby Blue
17.8	398	Wharf Rat*
18.4	66	Black Muddy River*
19.2	72	Knockin' on Heaven's Door*

Dead and Company		
Avg. Set Position	Times Played	Song Title
14.3	12	A Hard Rain's A-Gonna Fall
14.4	37	Standing on the Moon*
15.1	36	Touch of Grey
15.4	27	Days Between
15.5	33	Wharf Rat*
15.7	21	The Weight*
15.8	25	Black Peter*
16.0	36	Stella Blue*
16.2	11	Death Don't Have No Mercy
16.2	37	Morning Dew
16.6	26	Black Muddy River*
17.9	17	Knockin' on Heaven's Door*

Table 4. Average Set Position of Rousing Rockers for Grateful Dead and Dead and Company

Grateful Dead		
Avg. Set Position	Times Played	Song Title
18.1	417	Around and Around
18.2	661	Not Fade Away*
18.4	592	Sugar Magnolia*
19.0	301	Going Down the Road Feelin' Bad*
19.5	335	One More Saturday Night*
19.7	325	U.S. Blues*
20	281	Johnny B. Goode*

Dead and Company		
Avg. Set Position	Times Played	Song Title
14.2	29	Going Down the Road Feelin' Bad*
14.3	52	Casey Jones
14.5	20	Sugar Magnolia*
14.5	20	Turn on Your Lovelight
15.2	52	Not Fade Away*
15.5	47	One More Saturday Night*
16.9	49	U.S. Blues*
17.2	10	Johnny B. Goode*

CHARACTERISTICS OF SORROWFUL SONGS

There are some interesting common attributes among the set of songs that follow Space. The songs are mournful in tone. The characters in the song reflect deeply on the nature of their life, and they express regrets about the state that it is in. One example of lyrics is provided here, and readers are encouraged to research and determine for themselves whether these songs have a different mood then the typical easy-going, happy-go-lucky first set songs. The songs after Space all have a highly self-reflective mood, but they do not represent the whole song. Importantly, it is also a common element of each of these songs that they ultimately express hopefulness and an attitude of resolutely pursuing a positive approach to life.

"Stella Blue" has one of the quintessential statements of disillusionment:

> When all the cards are down
> There's nothing left to see
> There's just the pavement left
> And broken dreams[1]

For any concertgoer who has been following the band on a transcendent journey through Space, this is a hard sentiment to hear. Other songs immediately following Space express similar degrees of loss and regret. The song "Black Peter" is the somber meditation of a man who believes he is on his deathbed; the sentiments of "Knockin' on Heaven's Door" and "Death Don't Have No Mercy" similarly reflect the mortality that stalks each of us. In "Wharf Rat," a down-and-out stranger on the street makes a stirring vow to turn his life around. "Black Muddy River" was one of Garcia and Hunter's last collaborations, and it is a deep reflection on the disappointments that an idealistic person may encounter in this life, but again, like the other songs on this set, it reflects a determination to see it through.

The psychological terrain shifts dramatically during this block of the show. The mood during the Sorrowful Song can become downright morose, much as the mood during Space can be one of alienation. Not a few have wondered or expressed aloud during Space, Why are they putting us through this? A good answer might be found by analogy to other collective and ritualized activities. There are standardized practices in other communities in which there is a degree of discomfort for the participants. That discomfort is by design; it is not an unfortunate side effect but in fact a part of the plan. It is a feature not a bug, to borrow from IT terminology.

1. Robert Hunter and Jerry Garcia, "Stella Blue," Alfred Music, 1973.

Table 5. Liturgical Parallel for the Sequence of Sorrowful Songs and Rousing Rockers

	A	B	C
Dead Sequence	Space	Sorrowful Song	Rousing Rocker
Christian Liturgy	Examination of Conscience	Confession of Failings	Declaration of Pardon

The Deadhead trait: Deadheads look for the best in others.

The comment: Deadheads who recognize some aspects of their own life in the tales of woe told in second set songs come away from the concert unburdened, with a renewed lease on life. A crowd coming out of a Dead show after the set-two sequence of songs resemble nothing so much as a crowd emerging from a rousing, come-to-Jesus revival tent meeting. As a redeemed people, with faults acknowledged and after pledges to do better, they are ready to face whatever tomorrow brings with a renewed sense of joy in their heart. In that spirit, they are more apt to be accepting of others. And this is the essence of Scripture, instructing us in how we should interact with one another; for it is written, "Make sure no one repays a wrong with a wrong, but always pursue the good for each other and everyone" (1 Thess 5:15).

II

Self-reference in Songs

The passage: "It was in Antioch that they were first called Christians . . ." (Acts 11:26).

The context: For the writer of Acts to see a need to explain the origins of the use of the term "Christian" says something about the time of publication of that work. The implication is that it was an "in-between" time period. The term must have been in widespread use long enough for the audience to be interested to learn something about where it started. At the same time, they are not so far removed from events that memories cannot be drawn upon to sort out what happened where and when.

✝

The books selected for inclusion in the New Testament were written independently of one another (with the exception of Luke and Acts) and had completion dates spread over many decades. None of these witnesses were written as contemporaneous, newspaper-style reporting ("Three men charged with being troublemakers were executed outside Jerusalem yesterday") but instead were finalized long after the original events that they describe took place. They were all written with the knowledge, and in response to, a movement that was continuing to grow beyond any expectations. The later the completion date of the works (as understood today), the more the events described are presented and imbued with an interpretation of the ultimate meaning of what happened. John's Gospel is particularly notable for making clear in the narrative that all of the events described are of cosmic significance. Nothing happened that was not supposed to happen, and everything that did happen was part of the grand scheme. This was referenced in chapters 1 and 5 in relation to John's comments on Jesus' followers: in the first case that they would be known for their love; and in the second, that those who were believers without having seen Jesus for themselves would be considered fortunate.

NARRATIVE PERSPECTIVE IN ACTS

It is interesting to consider the conclusion to the Acts of the Apostles in light of its relatively late completion date. In the final scene, the apostle Paul is under house arrest in Rome. If, as lore and tradition tell us, he was executed there, it is not described in Acts. Or, to be more specific, it is not described in our surviving version of Acts. The narrative ends so abruptly, with Paul engaged in discourse with religious leaders, that readers have speculated for centuries whether the real ending might be missing. You could say the end is never told. The alternative explanation is that it was the writer's intention to leave it open-ended and ongoing: the narrative was not brought to an end because the story was not over.

How long it took the writer of Acts to complete that work is an interesting matter for speculation. It is clear that, when the action gets to Rome, the movement is well on its way to spreading to "all peoples" as was foretold at the end of part one—that is, Luke's Gospel. The movement is sufficiently well-established in Rome that those within the movement can be confident that it will continue to flourish for the foreseeable future. But was that outcome known when the early sections of Acts were being composed? The

ever intriguing "we" passages (e.g., 16:10–17, 27:1–8) give a contemporaneous, travel log feel to the story, suggesting that it was being composed as events unfolded. Or, alternatively, did the writer
assemble that whole narrative, going back through notes, with full
knowledge of how it would turn out?

The position of the New Testament writers, looking back to
document not only what happened but how and why, with full
knowledge that the movement had prospered, is very much like the
position of commentators on the Deadhead phenomenon today. It
would of course be outrageous to predict or expect a fan following
to continue for one hundred years, let alone one thousand, but today's observers can share this perspective with the New Testament
writers: the movement in question will continue to flourish for the
foreseeable future.

A PREVALENT THEME IN GRATEFUL DEAD LYRICS

The song lyrics composed by Robert Hunter have played a central
role in the Grateful Dead phenomenon, as was first mentioned in
chapter 7 in the context of the common attitudes and appetites of
Deadheads. The suggestion made there was that one of the contributors to the deeper level that Deadheads perceive when they
"get it" is that there are song lyrics that operate on many levels of
meaning.

One of those levels of meaning has to do with the significant
number of Hunter songs that refer to music, to songs and singing,
and to bands playing music. A sample of songs making such reference is found at the end of this chapter, and two are highlighted
here.[1] "Stella Blue" is one of the Sorrowful Songs referred to in the
previous chapter, and though it has a person's name in the title, it
is not about a character. Music references run through those lyrics,
including this one:

1. As noted earlier, the current practice of administering the copyrights to
song lyrics strongly discourages many quotations to be made in print; in this
chapter and the next, reference will be made to illustrative lyrics; readers are
encouraged to look them up for themselves.

> In the end there's just a song
> Comes crying up the night

Among the more jaunty songs that reference music and song is "Ramble on Rose." Near the end of a hodge-podge of cultural references is this line:

> I'm gonna sing you
> A hundred verses of ragtime[2]

Taken together with a collection of songs about a particular type of character (below), the lyrics about music constitute a recurring theme of self-reference. Throughout the ongoing development of the Grateful Dead world, Hunter commented on the very phenomenon of which he was a part and which he was helping to create.

From the earliest days of his involvement with the Grateful Dead, Hunter's lyrics were influenced by the unique atmosphere around the band. As a nonperforming member of the band (on several album jackets, Hunter is listed as lyricist), he responded in poetry while listening to the band explore its musical potential. Since he would not be the person out in front of the crowd singing the songs, he may have felt freer to comment on what the performers were doing, though without naming names. One line from "Stella Blue" was always a poignant self-reference at its origin and just continues to gain resonance in each decade in which it is performed:

> A broken angel sings from a guitar

In a later verse, another reference is made to musical performance, one which also plays on the emotions of fans who have heard it sung in concert for fifty years and must speculate on how many more times they will hear it:

> Dust off those rusty strings just one more time

That Hunter is referring to the band's collective, and unusual, experience is especially true in numerous songs that make specific

2. Robert Hunter and Jerry Garcia, "Ramble on Rose," Alfred Music, 1972.

reference to a band. Two in particular have become staples of the repertoire and are very frequently performed together in the same concert: "Uncle John's Band" and "Playin' in the Band." Bob Weir has now performed "Playin' in the Band" more than 1,100 times collectively in the concerts of the Grateful Dead, Ratdog, Furthur, Dead and Company, etc. and no one has any doubt about what type of band the song refers to. That song is also notable for including a line that will sound familiar to readers of Scripture, as it invites anyone who is without sin to cast criticism at the performers in the band.

THE PASSAGE OF TIME ADDS MEANING

The most autobiographical song about the band, though it never refers to a band or music, is one for which the band is best known: "Truckin.'" It has now been more than fifty years since Hunter penned the line that has been so-often quoted about the band's long journey. For this one, as much as for the other self-referential songs, the longevity of the performers' careers has imparted additional meaning to that line. They were only five years into what has now become a sixty-year odyssey when that comment was new, and it all just continues to get longer and stranger.

The lyrics to "Ramble on Rose" can provide suitable examples for many of the recurring themes in Robert Hunter's lyrics, including in the category of those lyrics that have gained meaning with the passage of time. Perhaps they were expressing hubris about their own abilities, or perhaps they were referring to a generic song and not their own individual effort, but the line "I know this song / It ain't never gonna end" becomes more interesting each year that it is performed. The extent to which the band has made manifest, by their longevity, that which they sang about, is more fully explored in the next chapter.

Of the many Hunter song lyrics that refer to songs, "Ripple" is one that has crossed over to recognition and enjoyment by a wide-range of music lovers. Many of Hunter's songs make passing reference to songs and music, but music itself is the principal subject of "Ripple." The last line before the chorus expresses a wish that there would be songs everywhere.

Each passing year and milestone adds significance to Hunter's lyrics about songs and music. At Dead and Company's first performance after the death of Hunter in 2019, the concert opened with "Ripple."[3] The first lines of that song, posing the question whether the poet could still expect to reach across time to move people, could not have been more poignant. Fifty years after the question was written, the crowd answered with a resounding yes. No poet could ask for more certain confirmation their message had been heard. (A side note about the hidden meanings to be found in each concert's setlist: all of the songs performed at that first show after Hunter's death were Robert Hunter compositions—something that would not have happened on a "normal" night. "Werewolves of London" as an encore was the sole exception—it being Halloween, after all).

RECURRING CHARACTERS

Beyond writing songs about songs and the band that performed them, Hunter also wrote a collection of songs about characters who share important attributes with Deadheads. (Though he never said that is what they were about; but then, he very rarely discussed what *any* set of lyrics was about.) In particular there are a set of songs with a common naming convention for the song title and the character. The convention is to have a two-word song title with a descriptor before a first name, often with alliteration. This convention is reminiscent of the sort of nicknames that were common in the world of the Merry Pranksters, and to a lesser degree the Hell's Angels, of the early Dead scene. This chapter will address "Cosmic Charlie," "Saint Stephen," "Ramble on Rose," and "Tennessee Jed." Two other songs with a similar naming convention illustrate recurring themes discussed in other chapters of this work.

3. The full setlist is available at Setlist.fm (https://www.setlist.fm/setlist/dead-and-company/2019/madison-square-garden-new-york-ny-539d2709.html).

Self-reference in Songs

"Black Peter" is one of the greatest of the mournful yet ultimately hopeful songs (previous chapter), and "Loose Lucy" includes a line that is significant in the crowd participation tradition (covered in the next chapter).

These songs are not the only ones that reflect a Deadhead's approach to life nor the only ones to revolve around a colorful personage. Together, though, they make a convenient set because they each reference a named character who share some common attitudes. That set of named-character songs contribute important elements to the full scope of what Hunter wrote about, much of which has been espoused by Deadheads as a philosophy of life. Simply stated, that attitude is one that Christians can relate to: finding reason for optimism in a world of calamity.

None of the characters in this set of songs has led an uncomplicated life, yet in each case an indomitable spirit remains. There is also a strain of grim practicality about Deadheads despite the common misperception that to be a Deadhead means to avoid ever having both feet on the ground. In reality, the traveling Deadheads who crisscross the country on a shoestring could not get by if they were entirely naïve to the ways of the cold cruel world; they know they must be on the lookout for trouble from any direction, as was Casey Jones, and that even when all seems safe and secure, you can't be too sure (Uncle John's Band).

"Tennessee Jed" is a song that crosses over from being about a character with a Deadhead sort of outlook to one that is a major crowd participation event (next chapter). The first lines of the song, however, make clear that this person's attitude does not come simply from wishing on rainbows, in that it starts with the wistful longings of an incarcerated person. "Saint Stephen" has also long been a crowd favorite, and one for which the meaning of some lines are different in the context of the ongoing phenomenon. As a character though, Saint Stephen is on that list of those for whom life has not been simple. It is clear that he has endured considerable losses, but that should never be cause for despair. "Cosmic Charlie" is one of the very earliest songs to describe the archetypal inhabitant of the Dead world, though it abounds with the incongruities and ambiguities that became Hunter's hallmarks. Despite the title that might be used as a stereotype for the detached hippie, among its final verses is reference to the sort of practicality that Deadheads, as well as everyone else, needs to get by in this world.

"Ramble on Rose" is another crowd favorite that has numerous references to songs and the band that brings them to life. It also touches on the slightly fatalistic but ultimately positive attitude about life that is the shared mind set of all Deadheads:

> The grass ain't greener
> The wine ain't sweeter
> Either side of the hill.

This chapter presents just a subset of the songs (those with named characters) of the many Hunter compositions that reflect a certain attitude toward life. In part these songs reflect the nature of the crowd that the Grateful Dead attracted, and in large part, Deadheads have been molded by these songs. The simplest description of that way of living is to say Deadheads recognize those moments when there is nothing left to do but smile.

$$\bigoplus$$

The Deadhead trait: Deadheads identify with the characters described in Grateful Dead songs.

The comment: It would be one thing for a carefree youth to identify with the characters described in Hunter's songs. For Deadheads to find new meaning in those songs as the decades pile up is a different sort of phenomenon. The longevity of this movement, not simply surviving now but thriving, heartens those who adopted that different way of life portrayed in the music. For a majority of a lifetime to have been lived while new wisdom was revealed by these songs is a powerful affirmation of the choices Deadheads made. The righteous, if occasionally hapless, heroes of these songs have been vindicated; it is now amply demonstrated that Saint Stephen will remain. An approach to life that is hopeful, even in full recognition of all the calamities life presents, including personal failings, is an approach described well in Scripture, including where it is written, "Live agreeably with one another; do not be arrogant but travel along with the lowly; do not come across as wiser than you are. Do not render anyone evil for evil, but give heed to what is pleasing in everyone's eyes. If it is possible, if it is up to you, live peaceably with all" (Rom 12:16–18).

SONGS WITH LYRICS THAT MAKE REFERENCE TO SONGS AND MUSIC

- "Brokedown Palace"
- "Ripple"
- "Bird Song"
- "Stella Blue"
- "Terrapin Station"
- "Uncle John's Band"
- "Candyman"
- "Dire Wolf"
- "Ramble on Rose"
- "Black Muddy River"
- "Attics of My Life"
- "Franklin's Tower"
- "Scarlet Begonias"
- "Deal"
- "Crazy Fingers"
- "Eyes of the World"

SONGS WITH LYRICS THAT MAKE REFERENCE TO A BAND

- "U.S. Blues"
- "Scarlet Begonias"
- "The Music Never Stopped"
- "Ramble on Rose"
- "Playing in the Band"
- "Sugar Magnolia"
- "Stella Blue"
- "Uncle John's Band"

SONGS WITH LYRICS MADE MORE SIGNIFICANT BY THE BAND'S LONGEVITY

- "Ramble on Rose"
- "The Music Never Stopped"
- "Brown-Eyed Women"
- "Stella Blue"
- "Estimated Prophet"
- "Not Fade Away"
- "Truckin'"
- "New Speedway Boogie"

12

Self-Actualization in
the Community

The passage: "Unto all Peoples . . ." (Luke 24:47).

The context: In concluding part one of his work, the writer of Luke and Acts makes an audacious claim: the gospel message that started amongst a small subset of Mediterranean enclaves could, should, and would reach across the entire globe. Even though the conception at that time of what constituted the "whole world" was far more limited than our current understanding, that writer's bold claim has still been proven true to a stunning degree.

$$\dagger$$

When the author of Luke and Acts wrote that the Jesus movement would spread to the ends of the world (Acts 1:8) and encompass all people (*ethne* in Greek), it was very bold indeed. It would have seemed a preposterous notion to the powerful people of that day that billions of believers for thousands of years would base their entire lives on those writings. If there were any who would even contemplate a unified human endeavor on that sort of scale, they likely would have expected it to be true for the Roman Empire, not for the fringe community in their midst who rejected the empire.

SHAPING THE FUTURE

There is a sort of intermission interposed by the writer between the end of Luke's Gospel and the beginning of Acts. Luke ends with Jesus' directive that they carry the word to all peoples, and Acts tells how that happened. A telling feature about the book of Acts is the *how* of the spread of the movement: there is very little active role attributed to God. The writer of Acts was very familiar with the Scripture writings that preceded Jesus' life, quoted them often, and knew of the frequent intervening of God's voice and action as an agent directing human affairs. That sort of interventions does not take place in Acts; the Spirit is acknowledged as the inspiration for what took place, but no divine voice is heard, nor does anything happen that is not the work of the apostles themselves (though Peter did converse with a divine voice while in a trance in the midday sun on a roof in Joppa [Acts 10:9-15]). They made manifest, by their writing and preaching, the movement that spread to all peoples.

In keeping with the premise of this book, that the Dead and Company time period is analogous to the period covered in Acts, this work must shift its focus to actions and events that relate to the future of the movement, not its past. Like the change in focus after the interval between part one and part two in Luke and Acts, we must now look at the propagation of the movement in a new way. Given the evidence that this remains an unfolding story, all that has been written about the history of the Grateful Dead as performers, in more than one hundred books and countless magazine articles, must now be considered in a new light. Which of those commentators perceived the forces that would carry this forward?

There have been recurring episodes in the past when fans were forced to contemplate the idea that there would be a "last Dead concert" (the hiatus in 1974, the coma in 1986, Garcia's death in 1995, the Fare Thee Well shows in 2015, and the "final" Dead and Company tour in 2023). After coming through these trials and tribulations, Deadheads today know with full certainty that there will be Dead shows, in some form or fashion, for the duration of their lives. With that assurance, all of the events, and especially the songs, of the past take on a different meaning, a meaning developed and made manifest by the Deadheads themselves.

PERFORMANCE INFORMED BY LONGEVITY

In the previous chapter, attention was drawn to song lyrics that have taken on new significance by virtue of the longevity of the Grateful Dead's performing career. This approach is also fruitful in looking at the second era of Dead performances through the 2020s, specifically those by the original performers. The new performers who have joined can also be interpreted with a more meaningful perspective when considered as contributors to something that has a future, not just a past.

For the original band members, some of the songs take on a new significance when interpreted as references to the dear departed Jerry Garcia. In the traditional marching song, "Peggy-O," a troop is being led off to battle when their captain becomes smitten with a lass in the town they are passing through. Alas, by the end of the song the captain is dead, his love unrequited. It is very easy to consider this song now as referring to Garcia as the captain and the maid as the muse that led him on. When performed now by Dead and Company, Bob Weir delivers some of his absolute most heartfelt singing on these phrases.

The song "Bird Song," originally written about the passing of Janis Joplin, is another that takes on added poignancy if heard as referring to Garcia. It takes only a slight rehearing of the pronouns in the first two lines to hear a lament for Garcia. That song also refers to a Deadhead's innate sense that the past moments of joy experienced in the music do not have to stay in the past, that the same sweet music once heard in the past can be heard again. This could just as well refer to the appeal that the fans find in the many shows done by Dead cover bands.

There are lyrics in many Dead songs that now take on new significance with the longevity of the phenomenon, but one will be quoted here as an example. "Stella Blue" has already been referred to in previous chapters as one of the most melancholy of the Sorrowful Songs, and one that is principally about music and songs, but it also contains a good deal of reflection about the life of performers. The last line "It seems like all this life was just a dream" cannot help but move the hearer in ways today that could only have been imagined when the same performers first presented it fifty years ago.

A prime example of a song that has shifted in meaning over the decades is also the song that catapulted the Grateful Dead into unexpected top ten exposure after twenty-two years of work: "Touch of Grey." The first heart-wrenching, self-revelatory moment came when that song was featured in concerts after Jerry Garcia returned to touring from being hospitalized with a diabetic coma. The refrain about survival had a resonance with the crowd that it simply could not have had prior to the health crisis that nearly ended Garcia's life, if not his performing career.

The layers of meaning being added to "Touch of Grey" did not end there. As the years rolled on and the successor bands came to the fore, including but not exclusively Dead and Company, the crowd joined in, full throated, when the words to the chorus shifted to a statement of collective survival. These words took on a significance not lost on anyone in the crowd. This was further heightened, and took on a significance no one would have asked for, when this song became the first one that Dead and Company performed when returning from the COVID pandemic hiatus.

PERFORMANCE INFORMED BY LEGACY

The original Grateful Dead songs were given a new significance when a songwriter and performer of the stature of John Mayer participated in concert tours over several years, and over hundreds of concerts into which he incorporated exactly none of his own music. Mayer has spoken in numerous interviews about the change in his outlook that came with being part of a band, and the special burden he feels to honor the memory of the performer whose role he now fills. Now, it is certainly true that any line to any given song can be reinterpreted to mean something that was not intended, but the emphasis that Mayer attaches to singing a line from "Sugaree" suggests that he wants the audience to know he attaches a unique personal meaning to the idea of his fame being subsumed in the collective. There is no doubt this one-time solo superstar feels a deep personal renewal in serving the greater Dead community or, as he has put it, "most importantly to be a part of something much bigger than myself."[1]

Another song Mayer puts great emotion into the performance of is "Black Muddy River," one of the last great songs that Garcia and Hunter wrote together. It is a deeply symbolic poem and always performed with due reverence and melancholy. The particular lines that take on new meaning when sung by one as accomplished as Mayer are the last lines. Mayer typically repeats these lines, about the singing of songs, several more times than was Garcia's practice. But to include any of his own songs—in fact, anything that was not in the canon of Dead songs—during a Dead and Company show is something that Mayer devoutly will not do. What does he mean, then, by emphasizing that line about a song of my own? Perhaps with his ego now so subsumed in the joint endeavor, he does consider this song to be "his own" though he did not compose it.

ROLE OF DEADHEADS AT THE SHOW

Even as the significance of song lyrics naturally has changed with the performers over the decades, the Deadheads have played a role in shaping what the music means. Apart from the community vibe that comes from joining, all as one, on the chorus of songs that

1. Wilkes, "John Mayer," para. 4.

mean so much on a personal level, there are a number of songs the crowd has come to play a role in during concerts. One such example also fits the category of what has already been discussed: songs that have taken on new meaning in the absence of Garcia.

"Ramble on Rose" has numerous self-referential points, as discussed in the previous chapter. One particular line takes on greater meaning with every performance: "I know this song it ain't never gonna end." Just as it did during the later years of the Grateful Dead's performing career, it is even more meaningful now when the senior citizen members of the band continue to declare its truth to full stadium crowds.

There is one line in that song, though, that exemplifies how the crowd has asserted itself into being part of the performance. Everyone in the crowd knows the line is coming and everyone prepares to shout their tribute to Garcia after the phrase "Take you to the leader of the band." With that line and others to be described, the musicians anticipate the reaction and are ready to hesitate and glide for a moment or two as the crowd plays out its part.

SONGS ABOUT THE SHOW

The crowd shapes the concert experience in ways beyond the expected sing-alongs and the reaction to favorite lines. There are a number of instances in which the lines of songs have changed meaning entirely through their association with the concert experience. The song "Loose Lucy" has nothing whatsoever to do with the concertgoing experience and yet the crowd has seized upon one line, which expresses gratitude for mutual time well-spent, as its own. The crowd lustily shouting out this line has everything to do with what the entire Deadhead experience means to them, and the performers duly give room for the crowd to express themselves.

There is another line that the crowd has now attached new meaning to with their roar of approval. This is a song that on the surface might be about the first flame of romance, though it could just as easily be interpreted as being about the band-and-Deadhead symbiosis. When the band now plays the song "Feel Like a Stranger," and sings a line about a show, the crowd claims the moment. In recognition of this, the drummers pound out a few beats to give the crowd their say before the instrumentalists resume the tune.

THE DEADHEADS' WORLD

The atmosphere of a live Dead concert has a significance for Deadheads that make most aspects of their routine lives pale by comparison. The exhilaration of the collective joy of being together once again attaches itself to particular phrases in certain songs. As a communal body, the crowd has made those phrases mean something specifically about their shared world.

The previous chapter has already introduced one of the songs that is a quintessential expression of the Dead world as a thing unto itself. The chorus of "Tennessee Jed" includes a repeated reference to Tennessee with a fond expression of longing to be there. The enthusiasm with which *every* Deadhead crowd sings along is not because they are all enamored of the Volunteer State. Rather, the name Tennessee stands in for the exalted state that Deadheads go to collectively. Another song referred to in the previous chapter has a line about the alternate universe inhabited by Deadheads. Near the end of "Saint Stephen" comes a line on which the band slows down so as to give the crowd space to shout out their declaration that the exalted state found at the show has gotten to feel like home. For Deadheads, singing along to that line is declaring the spiritual home they wish to occupy.

One final example will be offered of songs that represent the collective Deadhead homeland. "Terrapin Station" is a song (and album title) that came out in the middle of the Grateful Dead recording career. It was a significant departure in style and launched a creative era that is often cited as some of the best of their years of live concerts. The full set of lyrics for this are some of Robert Hunter's most evocative. The premise is that a train is advancing toward a destination, one that all Deadheads hope to reach, even though (or because) it has slightly mysterious air. The Deadhead concert crowd all knows, as one, when they have arrived at Terrapin.

NOT FADE AWAY

One of the most powerful examples of the fan community taking hold of a song and imbuing it with a new meaning related to themselves is "Not Fade Away." What started out as one of Buddy Holly's many impossibly catchy odes to teen romance has now become the enduring anthem of Deadheads everywhere. This number is one of the Rousing Rockers that brings the long second set to a close in exultation. It has now become standard and expected that the crowd will take over as the band winds down, clapping along to that distinctive beat and calling out, in alternation with the performers, that their shared love will go on without end. Eventually it becomes an audience-only clap-and-chant as the band leaves the stage, and it continues until they return for the encore.

This clap pattern has become one of the sure signs that the crowd has taken over the role of perpetuating the legacy of the band. Even after the more reflective encore, Deadheads will go out into the night and resume clapping the beat that they all recognize: in stairwells, on escalators, in parking garages, in underpasses, overpasses, shuttle buses, everywhere they are temporarily clustered as they make their way home. In doing so, they themselves manifest the legacy and the future: as long as there are others out there to clap along, then they have proof that the love they believed and hoped was real is now shown, absolutely and undeniably, to be so. Today they have no reason to fear that it will fade away.

THE FUTURE OF DEADHEADS

For a clear example of a Deadhead's attitude and actions to secure the future of the movement, consider again the case of John Mayer. Back in his early enthusiastic days as a new convert, he made a comment that at first would seem to be prescient. In truth, the comment was not just a prediction but a promise which he himself had a large role in fulfilling. As it can also serve now as a prediction for future decades, it is fitting that they be the last words of this work. In his January 2013 Rolling Stone interview, Mayer said, "Mark my words, the Grateful Dead are gonna make a comeback."[2]

$$\bigcirc\!\!\!\!\!f$$

The Deadhead trait: Deadheads are optimistic about the future of the movement (and in general).

The comment: The Deadhead phenomenon is still relatively new when compared to many sports franchises. Those organizations also require a rejuvenating fan base who will stay loyal even though the passing decades must necessarily include turnover in personnel and adjustments to the style of play. Deadheads, for their part, have demonstrated that they are in it for the long haul. A crucial distinction between the sports fan base and the Deadhead movement is the dominant role played by the owners of the sports franchise. There is no such entity in the Dead world. The fate of their movement remains, as it always has, in the Deadheads' hands. Thus far they have shown that they will be active in its propagation. In doing so, they will find it to be true what was written: "A bounty of righteousness is sown in peace by those making peace" (Jas 3:18), and further, while "no one has ever seen God, if we love each other, God abides in us" (1 John 4:12).

2. Doyle, "Mayer on His New Voice," para. 15.

Epilogue

When the writing of this work began, the summer of 2023 was set as the endpoint of the time period covered, coinciding with what was heralded as the final tour of Dead and Company. The range in the appeal of that tour was captured when, on the one hand, the band was referenced in congressional testimony by the Fed chairman. A few weeks later a photo was featured on the cover of *New York Times Sunday Magazine* of a young-ish person, who to all appearances would be the polar opposite of the Fed chair, blissfully dancing to the same music that the Fed chairman had praised. It seemed to be a suitable framing to capture a time period.

But nothing stays the same. In 2024, more events have taken place that further weave Dead influence into the mainstream culture. Dead and Company conducted a series of concerts in a new venue that in many ways represents an entirely new art form. At the Sphere in Las Vegas, the visual displays are easily an equal attraction to the musical performance taking place (not entirely unlike the Acid Test environments of nearly sixty years ago). And at the polar opposite of the Acid Test scene, the Grateful Dead are being honored by the Kennedy Center for their lifetime artistic achievement. Sadly, 2024 also saw the death of Phil Lesh, a founding member of the band, just before the Kennedy Center honor gala was held. *Lux perpetua luceat eis.*

Appendix A

Schema of Scripture Passages and Deadhead Traits, by Chapter

Chapter 1: Analogy		
"If it be of man it will fail, but if it be of God . . ." (Acts 5:38–39).	Deadheads have themselves said, or heard others say, that GD is like "my religion."	"Don't snuff out the Spirit. Do not disregard prophetic messages . . ." (1 Thess 5:19–20).
Chapter 2: Phenomenon		
"About three thousand were added on that day . . ." (Acts 2:41).	Deadheads value new experiences more highly than new possessions.	"Are any of you wise and understanding? Show that your actions are good with a humble lifestyle that comes from wisdom . . ." (Jas 3:13).
Chapter 3: Baseball		
"Whoever is not against us is for us . . ." (Mark 9:40).	Deadheads delight in meeting other Heads.	"Hold one another in brotherly love; take the lead in honoring one another . . ." (Rom 12:10).

Appendix

Chapter 4: Uniqueness		
"Many followed him, but were scattered when he died . . ." (Acts 5:37).	No one stops being a Deadhead.	"If there is any excellence and anything worthy of praise, think about these things . . ." (Phil 4:8).

Chapter 5: The New Now		
"The Spirit fell on them as it had on us at the beginning . . ." (Acts 11:15).	Deadheads love to hear new versions of their favorite songs.	"Wisdom from above that is first pure, peaceful, gentle, yielding, filled with mercy and good actions, fair, and sincere . . ." (Jas 3:17).

Chapter 6: Conversion		
"Last of all, as one untimely born . . ." (1 Cor 15:8).	Deadheads can describe, in detail, a concert (or listening experience) that was life-changing.	"The fruit of the Spirit is love, joy, peace, patience, kindness, goodness, faithfulness, gentleness, and self-control . . ." (Gal 5:22–23).

Chapter 7: Shared Attributes		
"Some believed the things which were spoken . . ." (Acts 28:24).	Deadheads all love to dance (though some do not dance to other music).	"Don't be slack in enthusiasm; let the Spirit boil over . . ." (Rom 12:11).

Chapter 8: Sinners and Outcasts		
"At that time a huge persecution began . . ." (Acts 8:1).	There are no mean Deadheads.	"Comfort the discouraged, help the weak, be patient with all . . ." (1 Thess 5:14).

Chapter 9: Signification		
"Greet all with a holy kiss . . ." (1 Thess 5:26).	Deadheads own GD merchandise not sold by the band.	"Be of the same mind, having the same love, being in full accord and of one mind . . ." (Phil 2:2).

Schema of Scripture Passages and Deadhead Traits, by Chapter

Chapter 10: Liturgy		
"Passing down to you that which I received . . ." (1 Cor 11:23).	Deadheads look for the best in others.	"Make sure no one repays a wrong with a wrong, but always pursue the good for each other and everyone . . ." (1 Thess 5:15).
Chapter 11: Self-Reference		
"It was in Antioch that they were first called Christians . . ." (Acts 11:26).	Deadheads identify with characters described in GD songs.	"Live agreeably with one another; do not be arrogant but travel along with the lowly; do not come across as wiser than you are . . ." (Rom 12:16).
Chapter 12: Self-Actualization		
"Unto all Peoples . . ." (Luke 24:47).	Deadheads are optimistic about the future of the movement (and in general).	"A bounty of righteousness is sown in peace by those making peace . . ." (Jas 3:18).

Appendix B

Online Resources

Dead.net—Official site of the band and online home of Deadheads
Deaddisc.com—Discography of recordings related to Bay Area music
Deadstudies.org—Grateful Dead Studies Association
Deadandcodb.com—Dead and Company database
Deadtracks.com—Database of every time a song was played
Gdao.org—Digitized content from the UC Santa Cruz Grateful Dead archive
GdSets.com—Newsletter archive, setlists, ticket stubs, concert posters
Gratefuldeadbook.com—Guidebook to setlists and performances
Gratefulsets.net—Searchable collection of dates, songs, and venues
Gratefulstats.com—Tool for searching songs (and venues, etc.) in combination
Guides.library.ucsc.edu/grateful-dead—Grateful Dead Research Guide at UC
    Santa Cruz Library
Herbibot.com—Grateful Dead setlists, streaming, video, statistics, history
Jerrybase.com—Database of Jerry's performances with GD and side bands
OtherOnes.net—Setlists for The Other Ones, The Dead, Furthur
PhilZone.com—Setlists for Phil Lesh projects through 2016
Ratdog.org—Setlists for Bob Weir bands
Relisten.net—Tool to facilitate finding recordings of particular dates
Setlist.fm—Setlists for bands currently touring, plus convenient statistics
Setlists.net—Searchable collection of dates, songs, and venues
Whitegum.com—Searchable lyrics (shows what one person's obsession can do)

Bibliography

Adams, Rebecca, and Robert Sardiello, eds. *Deadhead Social Science: You Ain't Gonna Learn What You Don't Wanna Know*. Walnut Creek, CA: AltaMira, 2000.

Backstrom, Melvin. "The Grateful Dead and Their World: Popular Music and the Avant-Garde in the San Francisco Bay Area, 1965–1975." PhD diss., McGill University, 2018.

Baiano Berman, Deborah J. "Deadheads as a Moral Community." PhD diss., Northeastern University, 2002.

Bassi, Margherita. "James Webb Telescope Confirms the Universe Is Expanding Faster Than We Thought—and Scientists Still Don't Know Why." *Smithsonian Magazine*, Dec. 13, 2024. https://www.smithsonianmag.com/smart-news/james-webb-telescope-confirms-the-universe-is-expanding-faster-than-we-thought-and-scientists-still-dont-know-why-180985622.

Benson, Michael. *Why the Grateful Dead Matter*. Lebanon, NH: University Press of New England, 2016.

Bones, Bobby. "John Mayer Talks New Album, Songs He Doesn't Like Playing and More." *Bobby Bones Show*, Aug. 8, 2017. https://bobbybones.iheart.com/featured/bobby-bones/content/2017-08-08-watch-john-mayer-talks-new-album-songs-he-doesnt-like-playing-more/.

Brackett, John. *Live Dead: The Grateful Dead, Live Recordings, and the Ideology of Liveness*. Durham, NC: Duke University Press, 2023.

Bradshaw, Geoffrey W. "Collective Expressions and Negotiated Structures: The Grateful Dead in American Culture, 1965–95." PhD diss., University of Wisconsin, 1997.

Brightman, Carol. *Sweet Chaos: The Grateful Dead's American Adventure*. New York: Clarkson N. Potter, 1998.

Browne, David. *So Many Roads: The Life and Times of the Grateful Dead*. New York: Da Capo, 2015.

Budnick, Dean. "Dead and Company: The Origin Story." *Relix*, July 14, 2023. https://relix.com/articles/detail/dead-and-company-the-origin-story.

Bibliography

Butrica, James. "The Medical Use of Cannabis Among the Greeks and Romans." *Journal of Cannabis Therapeutics* 2 (2002) 51–70.

The Capitol Theatre. "12 Unforgettable Moments at 'Fare Thee Well' in Chicago." *The Squirrel* (blog), July 7, 2015. https://www.thecapitoltheatre.com/blog/detail/12-unforgettable-moments-at-fare-thee-well-in-chicago.

Conners, Peter. *Growing Up Dead: The Hallucinated Confessions of a Teenage Deadhead*. New York: Da Capo, 2009.

———. *JAMerica: The History of The Jam Band Scene, from the Grateful Dead to Phish to H.O.R.D.E to Bonnaro, and Beyond*. Boston: Da Capo, 2013.

Culli, Daniel R. "Never Could Read No Road Map: Geographic Perspectives on the Grateful Dead." MS diss., Louisiana State University, 2004.

Dawson, Daniel K. "Golden Roads and Unlimited Devotion: Following the Grateful Dead as Religious Pilgrimage." MA diss., San Diego State University, 2020.

Delray, Dean. "John Mayer/Part 1." *Let There Be Talk*, Nov. 4, 2019. https://deandelray.libsyn.com/podcast/2019/11.

Dodd, David, and Diana Spaulding, eds. *The Grateful Dead Reader*. New York: Oxford University Press, 2002.

Dodd, David, and Robert Weiner. *The Grateful Dead and the Deadheads: An Annotated Bibliography*. Westport, CT: Greenwood, 1997.

Doyle, Patrick. "John Mayer on His New Voice, Summer Tour and Dating Katy Perry." *Rolling Stone*, Jan. 30, 2013. https://www.rollingstone.com/music/music-news/qa-john-mayer-on-his-new-voice-summer-tour-and-dating-katy-perry-176802.

Gans, David. *Conversations with the Dead: The Grateful Dead Interview Book*. New York: Da Capo, 2002.

Gans, David, and Peter Simon. *Playing in the Band: An Oral and Visual Portrait of the Grateful Dead*. New York: St. Martin's, 1985.

Garcia, Jerry. "Jerry Garcia—1983 June 2nd—Complete Interview—MTV Studios, NY." LoloYodel. Uploaded on Dec. 29, 2016. YouTube video, 30:03. https://www.youtube.com/watch?v=sN4E5GQIZao.

Gaventa, Beverly Roberts. Introduction to *Acts of the Apostles*. In *The HarperCollins Study Bible: Fully Revised and Updated*, edited by Wayne A. Meeks, 2056–58. New York: HarperCollins, 2006.

GDSets.com. "GD Newsletter 1967." https://gdsets.com/images/periodicals/periodicals.htm.

Grushkin, Paul, et al. *The Official Book of the Deadheads*. New York: Quill, 1983.

Fricke, David. "John Mayer on Playing with Dead and Company: 'It's Like Catching Air.'" *Rolling Stone*, June 21, 2016. https://www.rollingstone.com/music/music-news/john-mayer-on-playing-with-dead-company-its-like-catching-air-153950.

Halperin, Shirley. "John Mayer Talks Grateful Dead Legacy, Fare Thee Well and Learning to Play 'A Universe of Great Songs.'" *Billboard*, Aug. 5, 2015. https://www.billboard.com/music/music-news/john-mayer-grateful-dead-and-company-interview-6655956.

Bibliography

Harrison, Hank. *The Dead: A Social History of the Grateful Dead.* New York: Links, 1973.

———. *The Dead.* Millbrae, CA: Celestial Arts, 1980.

Hunt, Pamela. "Where the Music Takes You: A Symbolic Interactionist View of Nomadic Vendors in a Music Scene." MA diss., Ohio University, 2002.

Jackson, Blair. *Garcia: An American Life.* New York: Viking, 1999.

———. *Goin' Down the Road: A Grateful Dead Traveling Companion.* New York: Harmony, 1992.

———. *Grateful Dead: The Music Never Stopped.* New York: Delilah, 1983.

Jackson, Blair, and David Gans. *This Is All a Dream We Dreamed: An Oral History of the Grateful Dead.* New York: Flatiron, 2015.

Jarnow, Jesse. *Heads: A Biography of Psychedelic America.* New York: Da Capo, 2016.

Kaler, Michael. "Ensemble Stuff: The Grateful Dead's Development of Rock-Based Improvisational Practice and Its Religious Inspiration." PhD diss., York University, 2014.

Kelly, Linda. *Deadheads: Stories from Fellow Artists, Friends, and Followers of the Grateful Dead.* New York: Citadel, 1995.

Kreutzmann, Bill. *Deal: My Three Decades of Drumming, Dreams, and Drugs with the Grateful Dead.* New York: St. Martin's, 2015.

Lehman, Alan R. "Music as Symbolic Communication: The Grateful Dead and Their Fans." PhD diss., University of Maryland, 1994.

Lesh, Phil. *Searching for the Sound: My Life with the Grateful Dead.* New York: Little, Brown, 2005.

Longcroft-Wheaton, Octavius. "The Stylistic Development of the Grateful Dead: 1965–1973." PhD diss., University of Surrey, 2020.

Malvinni, David. *Grateful Dead and the Art of Rock Improvisation.* Lanham, MD: Scarecrow, 2013.

McClain, Jordan. "Media Framing as Brand Positioning: Analysis of Coverage Linking Phish to the Grateful Dead." PhD diss., Temple University, 2011.

McNally, Dennis. *A Long Strange Trip: The Inside History of the Grateful Dead.* New York: Three Rivers, 2003.

Myler, Ariel G. "The Music Never Stopped: Tradition and Transformation in the Deadhead Community." MA diss., University of Oregon, 2021.

Neal, Jeff. "Up in Smoke?" *Harvard Law Today,* Sept. 5, 2023. https://hls.harvard.edu/today/harvard-law-expert-explains-federal-governments-push-to-ease-marijuana-restrictions.

Reeder, Nicholas Clark. "The Co-Evolution of Improvised Rock and Live Sound: The Grateful Dead, Phish, and Jambands." PhD diss., Brown University, 2014.

Richardson, Peter. *No Simple Highway: The Cultural History of the Grateful Dead.* New York: St. Martin's, 2015.

Robertson, Ray. *All the Years Combine: The Grateful Dead in Fifty Shows.* Windsor, ON: Biblioasis, 2023.

Bibliography

Roeloffs, Mary Whitfill. "A Deadhead at Heart? Fed Chair Powell Confirms Visit to Virginia Dead and Co. Show." *Forbes*, June 21, 2023. www.forbes. com/sites/maryroeloffs/2023/06/21/a-deadhead-at-heart-fed-chair-powell-confirms-visit-to-virginia-dead--co-show/.

Ruhlmann, William. *The History of the Grateful Dead*. New York: Gallery, 1990.

Sawyer, Peter. "A Qualitative Examination of the Ritual Structure and the Spiritual Nature of the Grateful Dead Experience." PhD diss., California School of Integral Studies, 2003.

Scully, Rock, and David Dalton. *Living with the Dead: Twenty Years on the Bus with Garcia and the Grateful Dead*. New York: Little, Brown, 1996.

Shenk, David, and Steve Silberman. *Skeleton Key: A Dictionary for Deadheads*. New York: Broadway, 1994.

Smith, Stacy L. "Dead and Still Grateful: Deriving Mechanisms of Social Cohesion from Deadhead Culture." PhD diss., Kansas State University, 2017.

Sylvan, Robin. *Traces of the Spirit: The Religious Dimensions of Popular Music*. New York: New York University Press, 2002.

Trager, Oliver. *The American Book of the Dead: The Definitive Grateful Dead Encyclopedia*. New York: Simon & Schuster, 1997.

Tuedio, Jim, and Stan Spector, eds. *The Grateful Dead in Concert: Essays on Live Improvisation*. Jefferson, NC: McFarland, 2010.

Wilkes, Emma. "John Mayer Says Being in Dead and Company Has Made Me a Better Player." Guitar.com. July 20, 2023. guitar.com/news/music-news/john-mayer-says-playing-in-dead-and-company-made-him-better-player.

Wood, Brent. *The Tragic Odes of Jerry Garcia and the Grateful Dead: Mystery Dances in the Magic Theater*. New York: Routledge, 2020.

Wren, Adam. "Eli Lilly's Hazy Memory." *Indianapolis Monthly*, Mar. 19, 2019. https://www.indianapolismonthly.com/longform/eli-lillys-hazy-memory-marijuana.

www.ingramcontent.com/pod-product-compliance
Lightning Source LLC
Chambersburg PA
CBHW060400090426
42734CB00011B/2195